COMPLETE COOKBOOK FOR INFRA-RED BROILER AND ROTISSERIE

Drawings by H. Lawrence Hoffman

complete

cookbook for

infra-red

broiler

and rotisserie

NEDDA CASSON ANDERS

M. Barrows and Company, Inc.
Publishers   New York

for
George
who
tasted
and
approved

PART I

THE INFRA-RED BROILER

PART II

THE ROTISSERIE

the

infra-red

broiler

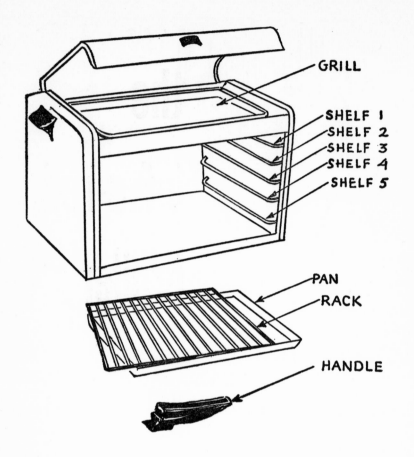

GRILL

SHELF 1
SHELF 2
SHELF 3
SHELF 4
SHELF 5

PAN
RACK

HANDLE

about the infra-red broiler

Your modern table broiler is a versatile and wonderful cooking appliance. Functional as well as beautiful, it fits today's requirements for casual eating, better meals, more comfortable living.

THE TABLE BROILER HAS MANY ADVANTAGES

It is portable. Think of the convenience of cooking dinner in an appliance handsome enough for the dining table in your city apartment. Of serving cocktail hors d'oeuvre from a cart wheeled to the terrace in the country. Of having cooking facilities in a one-room apartment with no kitchen. You can serve hot food anywhere you like: grilled sandwiches in the television den, shish kebabs in the living room, wiener broils for teen-agers in the rumpus room. You can even plug in the broiler near your outdoor barbecue and use it for supplementary cooking.

It is worksaving. A minimum of parts, most of them stainless steel and chromium, can be quickly washed. Waist-high operation keeps food always visible, eliminates stooping and oven peeking.

It is timesaving. Mixed grills can be done quickly. You will find many suggestions in this book for good go-togethers. Use the broiler top for heating bread, biscuits, rolls. Melt butter, warm serving platters, in the bottom. You can actually serve a complete dinner *minutes* after you turn on the switch. Some broilers even have an automatic timing device which rings a bell and turns off the heat when a meal is done, so you can cook without being in the room.

Your kitchen is always smokeless and cool. Smoke, caused by accumulated grease and improper air circulation, is eliminated. Grease spatters are burned off by the intense heat, and air flows properly into the open broiler. Because you heat a small, compact, quick-cooling appliance, instead of a large oven, your kitchen remains comfortable even in summer.

Broiled food is healthful and flavorful. Broiling is a healthful cooking method, since foods best retain vitamins and minerals when cooked quickly and without water or fat.

Juices are actually *sealed in* by infra-red rays, and a delicious flavor is the result.

It is versatile. From breakfast, through luncheon and dinner, any meal for big or little families can be prepared in the table broiler. And almost any food can be broiler-cooked: eggs, fish, fowl, meat, many vegetables, also fruit.

And it really broils. Broiling is cooking by direct heat. It is probably the easiest, oldest, and perhaps the most popular way of preparing food. In many broilers, food is cooked by the heat which surrounds it. But in fast, radiant, infrared broilers with an open front, cooking is by direct heat . . . which is true broiling.

HOW TO CARE FOR YOUR NEW APPLIANCE

Most infra-red broilers are guaranteed for one year, some for two, against electrical and mechanical defects, and parts are usually replaced without charge. Here are suggestions to help your broiler give you the best service:

1. Follow the manufacturer's directions. Read them carefully, then paste them in this book, page 206, where they will be always available.

2. Place your broiler on a convenient, level, dry table (preferably one with wheels) or on a counter. Uneven surfaces may result in a fall that will put your broiler out of commission. Wet electric cords invite injury to you as well as to equipment.

3. Disconnect the broiler after each use. As soon as it has cooled slightly, soak tray and rack in warm, soapy water. Wipe the inside, if it needs it, with a damp cloth and warm soapy water. Wipe again with a cloth wrung out of clear hot water, and dry thoroughly. *Do not wash the heating coils;* any spattered grease will be burned off by the intense heat. *Never immerse your broiler in water.*

4. Occasionally use a silver or chrome metal polish if it is necessary to restore your broiler to its original luster. Follow the manufacturer's directions.

5. Do not use other appliances on the same circuit at the same time; avoid overloading. Check the directions to be sure you are using the proper current. Most broilers operate on AC (alternating current); some also operate on DC (direct current).

HOW TO USE YOUR BROILER

1. Turn on the switch and preheat the broiler as the manufacturer directs; usually 4 to 10 minutes. If the manufacturer does not recommend preheating, add a few minutes to broiling time. To save washing, line pan with aluminum foil. Grease the pan or rack; then preheat it or not, as you wish.

2. Arrange lean food in the broiler pan, but place fat foods on the broiler rack in the pan so that fat can drain off.

3. Remove the broiler rack when it is not in use.

4. Place the pan on shelf. Rest handle outside, or take it off. The shelf nearest the heating coils is called the 1st shelf.

Just below is the 2nd shelf, and so on. If the distances and shelf positions given in these recipes do not suit your broiler, follow distance directions only. Distance is measured from broiling pan to heating coils, not from top of food to heating coils.

5. If your appliance has more than one heat, use high heat for broiling and low heat to keep foods warm if there is a delay in serving.

6. Do not use the spatter shield when broiling. The open front cools the air surrounding the food; this is desirable in broiling.

7. Heat plates and serving platter in the bottom of the broiler during the last few minutes of cooking.

8. To cook where you please, set the broiler on a tray large enough to hold baster, tongs, spatula, lemon wedges, butter plate, condiments, etc. Prepare ahead in the kitchen as much as you can—shape the hamburgers, top the tomatoes, fill the peaches—then at the last minute arrange the food on the pan, start the cooking, and you remain unflurried.

A serving cart or buffet on wheels, with at least two shelves, is functional and decorative too. Use the top shelf to hold the equipment tray, and as a working surface; the lower shelf is made to order for silver and serving dishes, as well as coffee cups. Some servers have leaves which can be raised for intimate dining.

9. Cooking times are necessarily approximate, since voltage, appliances, and foods vary. So do cook to your own taste.

USEFUL ACCESSORIES

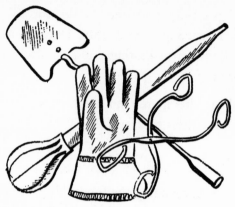

Aluminum foil saves washing. *Aluminum foil cups* or small *ovenware cups* are fine in which to heat already cooked vegetables, sauces, and gravies. Inexpensive *metal baking sheets, pie plates*, and *casseroles* in various sizes are best for small amounts of food and save washing a large pan. Very useful are: *skewers* of various lengths for shish kebabs, one or two *planks* for planking meats, fish, and chicken, a *pastry brush*, and a *bulb-and-ovenware-glass baster* for basting. An *asbestos glove*, a *spatula* with a metal or wood, not plastic, handle, *tongs*, and a *metal fork* make it easy to remove food from a hot broiler.

THE GRILL

If your broiler has a grill, use it as a warming plate for vegetables, and coffee; to grill tomatoes, fry bacon and eggs; heat serving platters, melt butter, and toast bread.

hot appetizers, sandwiches, and snacks

They are so much better in the broiler! Those little savory snacks that come fresh and hot, ready as wanted, from your table broiler set up in the living room, on the terrace, or in the rumpus room. How many steps you save when you can watch the cooking and enjoy the party too, instead of running back and forth to the kitchen range, many steps and many bends away.

Your family will cheer the sandwiches. They are just right for hungry youngsters after winter sports, or for everybody on warm summer days when one hot dish must be prepared. And how make-ahead sandwiches, to toast as needed, will appeal to your husband when he and his cronies take over the den and want no ladies present!

Broiler-made appetizers, sandwiches, and snacks mean more fun—and much less work for you. Try them any time, anywhere that good hot fare is the short order of the day.

HOT CANAPÉS ARE A TREAT

Dainty little oddments can bring new luster to your meals. Serve them not only as cocktail snacks in the living room, but to perk up soup or salad courses at the table. Shop the grocery stores for new bread and cracker bases, which come and go on the market too frequently to list here.

1.   AMERICAN CHEESE BITES

2-4 minutes in preheated broiler

About 5" from heat (3rd shelf in most broilers)

Spread buttered saltines with grated American cheese, or use a snappy cheese spread. Broil until cheese melts. Top with chopped olives or peanuts, and serve hot.

2.   ANCHOVY FINGERS

2-4 minutes in preheated broiler

About 5" from heat (3rd shelf in most broilers)

Cut white bread into fingers 1 inch wide, remove crusts, and toast one side. Place 2 flat anchovies on untoasted side. Top with grated Parmesan cheese. Broil until cheese melts.

3.   CHEESE PUFFS

2-4 minutes in preheated broiler

About 5" from heat (3rd shelf in most broilers)

Beat 1 egg white stiff. Blend in ½ cup mayonnaise and 1 package (3 ounces) cream cheese. Pile on 30 toast rounds, sprinkle with paprika, and broil until puffed and browned.

4. CRUNCHY CRAB MEAT

3-5 minutes in preheated broiler

About 5" from heat (3rd shelf in most broilers)

Mix 2 parts flaked crab meat with 1 part finely-chopped walnuts. Moisten with mayonnaise, season with salt and pepper, blend, and spread on triangles of toast. Brown lightly in the broiler.

5. HAM-PEANUT SPREAD

2-4 minutes in preheated broiler

About 5" from heat (3rd shelf in most broilers)

Chop fine equal parts of cooked ham and salted peanuts. Add salad oil to make right consistency and spread on rounds of Melba toast. Brown lightly in broiler.

6. MIXED DIAMONDS

2-4 minutes in preheated broiler

About 5" from heat (3rd shelf in most broilers)

Spread ground cooked shrimp, smoothed with butter and lemon juice, over half the surface of each toast diamond. (You can shape toast easily with sharp knife or cooky cutter.) Spread the other half with butter mixed with finely-chopped chives. Lay a strip of pimiento between the two spreads to mark the division. Heat in broiler.

7.   MUSHROOM MOUNDS

2-4 minutes in preheated broiler

About 5" from heat (3rd shelf in most broilers)

Spread Swedish rye bread or crisp crackers with seasoned, creamed mushrooms. Pile high in the center and sprinkle with dried parsley. Heat in broiler until bubbly.

8.   POTATO TIDBITS

2-4 minutes in preheated broiler

About 5" from heat (3rd shelf in most broilers)

Lay a thin, cooked potato slice on a round buttered cracker. Top with grated Cheddar cheese and a whiff of garlic salt, and broil until cheese browns lightly.

9.   ROLLED LIVER SNACKS

2-4 minutes in preheated broiler

About 5" from heat (3rd shelf in most broilers)

Grind 2 parts cooked chicken livers with 1 part hard-cooked egg; add onion juice, salt, and pepper to taste. Spread on buttered slices of white bread (crusts removed), and roll. Refrigerate for an hour or two; then butter outsides. Slice ½ inch thick, and broil, turning once, until lightly browned on both sides. Insert picks for easy serving.

10. TWO-CHEESE ROUNDS

2-4 minutes in preheated broiler

About 5" from heat (3rd shelf in most broilers)

Pile softened cream cheese on each buttered toast round, cover with a slice of American cheese trimmed to fit, and broil until cheese melts.

11. TWO-TIER TRIANGLES

2-4 minutes in preheated broiler

About 5" from heat (3rd shelf in most broilers)

Broiler-toast triangles of bread on one side. Spread the untoasted sides of half the triangles with prepared mustard and top with grated American cheese. Spread the rest of the triangles with a deviled tongue or ham spread. Heat all triangles under broiler. To serve, place a cheese triangle on top of a tongue or ham triangle, spread-side up.

HOT HORS D'OEUVRE AS YOU LIKE THEM

These luscious hors d'oeuvre are listed according to broiling time, so select a few from each group, fix them ahead, then set the broiler on the buffet table and broil them in batches as needed. For an attractive platter select hors d'oeuvre of different colors, different shapes.

3-5 minutes in preheated broiler

About 5" from heat (3rd shelf in most broilers)

12. BACON CRISPS

Spread raw half bacon slices with a snappy cheese spread. Roll up and secure with picks. Broil until crisp. Turn once.

13. LOBSTER CHUNKS

Dip cooked lobster chunks in melted butter or margarine; then roll in paprika. Broil until brown. Serve hot on picks. Prepare scallops or other sea food the same way.

3-5 minutes in preheated broiler

About 5" from heat (3rd shelf in most broilers)

14. PIGS ON A SKEWER

Roll a whole or a half bacon slice around any of the following. String on skewers, and broil until bacon is crisp. Turn once. To serve, lay skewers on plates and push food off with a sweep of the knife.

Thick banana slices   *Pineapple chunks*
Cubes of broiled liver   *Mashed-potato balls*
Cubes of any cooked meat *Prunes filled with nuts*
Cooked mushrooms   *Cubes of Swiss cheese*
Large stuffed olives   *Tomato wedges*
Drained oysters

15. NUT-STUFFED OLIVES

Stuff large green or ripe pitted olives with walnuts or pecans. Heat and serve on colored picks.

16. PARTY POTATO CHIPS

Sprinkle chips with garlic salt or brush with melted butter seasoned with dill seeds. Heat in broiler.

17. SALAMI STICKS

Spread thin slices of salami with Roquefort or blue cheese. Roll each slice around an Italian bread stick, leaving 1 inch of bread stick exposed at each end to serve as a handle. Secure with pick. Heat in broiler.

5-8 minutes in preheated broiler

About 5" from heat (3rd shelf in most broilers)

18. FRANKS ON A PICK

Slice franks into 1-inch pieces. Spear each piece with a pick. Dip one cut end in mustard, the other in catsup. Brown in broiler and serve on picks.

19. HOT RED CAPS

Remove stems from mushrooms and dip caps in melted butter or oil. Broil, hollow-side down for about 1 minute. Combine 2 parts minced smoked salmon and 1 part onion. Fill mushroom hollows with this mixture, sprinkle heavily with paprika, and return to broiler for 2 minutes longer, or until hot. (Chop mushroom stems and use in Recipe 22.)

20. MIDGET MEAT BALLS

Shape well-seasoned hamburgers, Recipe 79, into balls about 1 inch in diameter. Broil. Turn once. Serve on picks.

21. SALTED ALMONDS

5-8 minutes in preheated broiler

About 5" from heat (3rd shelf in most broilers)

Blanch and dry almonds or other nuts. Salt them, place in broiler pan, and broil until light brown. Turn once. Remove and let cool for a few minutes to make crisp before serving. (If you prefer oilier salted nuts, use 1 tablespoon butter for each cup of nuts.)

22. STUFFED SMALL TOMATOES

8-12 minutes in preheated broiler

About 5" from heat (3rd shelf in most broilers)

Select small oval (egg) tomatoes of similar size. Cut off stem end, scoop out pulp, and drain by inverting tomatoes for a few minutes. Season insides with salt and pepper. Fill with creamed chopped mushroom stems, chopped cooked ham, or any leftover cooked meat, and broil until tomatoes are tender.

23. HOW TO REHEAT BREAD

2-5 minutes in cold or preheated broiler

5"-7" from heat (3rd or 4th shelf in most broilers)

Almost any bread can be freshened under the broiler. Place slices or rolls on the lowest shelf and heat for a few minutes.

24. HOT SEASONED BREAD

2-5 minutes in cold or preheated broiler

5"-7" from heat (3rd or 4th shelf in most broilers)

Slice diagonally a large loaf of Italian, French, Vienna, or rye bread—almost through to the bottom. Between slices, spread softened butter well mixed with mashed garlic (or grated Parmesan cheese). Or use any of the spreads in Recipes 27 and 28. Heat under the broiler. Serve piping hot. A crunchy bread can be the making of a meal!

25. TOAST CUPS

3-5 minutes in preheated broiler

5"-7" from heat (3rd or 4th shelf in most broilers)

Cut crusts from bread slices, spread one side with soft butter, and press buttered side to fit into muffin pan. Brush top sides with butter and broiler-toast on a low shelf until golden brown. Use instead of patty shells.

26. CROUTONS

2-3 minutes in preheated broiler

About 5" from heat (3rd shelf in most broilers)

Remove crusts from slices of stale bread. Cut into 1-inch cubes, brush with melted butter, and broiler-toast on a low shelf, turning as necessary, until golden. Watch carefully as these burn quickly.

27. SWEET TOASTS

2-6 minutes in cold or preheated broiler

About 5" from heat (3rd shelf in most broilers)

Your table broiler can toast 6 to 8 bread slices at once—handy when you are making several sandwiches or preparing sweet toasts for breakfast or tea. For dainty service, cut bread into fancy shapes with cooky cutters, or, with a sharp knife, into strips, points, diamonds, or oblongs. Remove crusts, toast bread on one side, then spread any of the following on untoasted side, and heat in broiler. Preheat broiler, and use high shelf, for moist toast. Start in cold broiler and use low shelf, for dry toast.

Equal parts creamed butter and honey, sprinkling of grated orange peel

Equal parts creamed butter and apricot jam

Creamed butter mixed with cinnamon and sugar

Apple butter blended with maple sirup

4

44

28. HERB-SEASONED TOASTS

2-6 minutes in cold or preheated broiler

About 5" from heat (3rd shelf in most broilers)

Your family will love these seasoned toasts served with fish or meat. Follow Recipe 27, but spread with any of the following seasonings creamed *with butter:* caraway, celery seed, chili powder, dill seed, grated lemon rind, parsley, paprika, pimiento. Check your spice and herb shelf for other possibilities, and do experiment.

29. LOTS OF FRENCH TOAST

5-8 minutes in preheated broiler

About 5" from heat (3rd shelf in most broilers)

3-6 servings

2 eggs slightly beaten
1 cup milk
¼ teaspoon salt
6 slices bread

(Better allow for extras. Serve with honey or fruit jam)

Mix together eggs, milk, and salt. Soak one slice of bread at a time in mixture, for about 1 minute; then lay in well-buttered broiler pan and broil until golden brown. Butter pan again, turn toast with spatula, and broil until done. Isn't it nice to have this much French toast made at one time?

30. APRICOT SANDWICH TREAT

5-8 minutes in preheated broiler

About 5" from heat (3rd shelf in most broilers)

Cook dried apricots until soft, sweeten to taste, then put through food chopper. If not thick enough to spread, return to heat, cook until proper consistency is reached, and cool. Add a little grated nutmeg and spread on slices of white bread. Make sandwiches, butter outsides, and broiler-toast both sides. Serve piping hot.

31. PECAN-MUSHROOM SPREAD

6-8 minutes in preheated broiler

About 5" from heat (3rd shelf in most broilers)

6 sandwiches

1 can (3 or 4 ounces) chopped mushrooms, drained
1 tablespoon butter
½ cup chopped pecans
1 tablespoon mayonnaise
⅛ teaspoon salt
Dash pepper
6 slices processed American cheese
12 slices white bread

(Or use almonds or walnuts instead of pecans)

In a saucepan, brown mushrooms in butter. Combine with pecans and mayonnaise. Season with salt and pepper. Spread mixture on 6 bread slices. Make sandwiches, butter outsides, and broiler-toast both sides, turning once with spatula.

32. EGGS IN A NEST

8-10 minutes in preheated broiler

About 3" from heat (2nd shelf in most broilers)

4 servings

Split 4 English muffins, scoop out center dough, and spread softened butter in hollow. Place each one on a square of aluminum foil about 5 by 5 inches. Cup the foil around each muffin half. Broiler-toast lightly for about 2 minutes. Now drop an egg into each hollowed muffin, and return to broiler until eggs are as firm as you like them. Remove foil. Serve 2 nests for each portion.

33. EGG, ANCHOVY, AND MUSHROOM SANDWICH

4-6 minutes in preheated broiler

About 5" from heat (3rd shelf in most broilers)

For each sandwich, mash 1 hard-cooked egg, 1 tablespoon cooked sliced mushrooms, and add soft butter to moisten. Season with salt and pepper. Spread on bread slice, add 1 minced anchovy, cover with bread. Butter outsides and broiler-toast both sides. Serve hot.

34. CHEESEBURGERS FOR 6

8-12 minutes in preheated broiler

About 5" from heat (3rd shelf in most broilers)

6 servings

¾ pound ground beef
½ teaspoon salt
⅛ teaspoon pepper
6 slices processed American cheese
6 hamburger buns

(For Saturday night get-togethers and any-day hearty appetites)

Lightly mix together ground beef, salt, and pepper. Shape into 6 flat patties. Broil on one side for about 4 minutes, turn, and brown other side. Top with cheese slice, and continue broiling until cheese is melted. Serve on split, buttered, broiler-toasted hamburger buns. When cheeseburgers are done, pop hamburger buns in the broiler for a minute or two.

TELEVISION SNACK

Cheeseburgers for 6. Recipe above.
Tomato Wedges. Cut tomatoes into sections, season with salt and pepper, dip in buttered crumbs, and broil, without turning, alongside cheeseburgers.

35. ANYTHING-AND-CHEESE SANDWICH

4-6 minutes in preheated broiler

About 5" from heat (3rd shelf in most broilers)

Broiler-toast slices of bread on one side. Butter untoasted side, and cover with almost any leftover: sliced or chopped cooked chicken, turkey or ham, shrimps, flaked fish or vegetables. Top with 1 slice processed American cheese. Broil until cheese melts. Try different seasonings: caraway, chili powder, curry, paprika, or prepared mustard.

36. GRILLED AMERICAN CHEESE OPEN SANDWICH

4-6 minutes in preheated broiler

About 5" from heat (3rd shelf in most broilers)

Broiler-toast slice of pumpernickel bread on one side. Cover untoasted sides with slices of processed American cheese. Spread lightly with prepared mustard. Heat in broiler until cheese melts. For variety, cover cheese, before broiling, with raw bacon, cut into 1-inch pieces, or spread with chili sauce.

37. HOT CRAB-MEAT SANDWICH

4-6 minutes in preheated broiler

About 5" from heat (3rd shelf in most broilers)

To flaked crab meat, fresh cooked or canned, add grated onion and minced celery, mayonnaise, salt and pepper to taste. Spread on slices of bread, make sandwiches, butter outsides, and broiler-toast both sides.

38. CURRIED CREAM CHEESE AND CHIVE SANDWICH

4-6 minutes in preheated broiler

About 5" from heat (3rd shelf in most broilers)

6 sandwiches

Blend 1 package (3 ounces) cream cheese and 2 table-spoons chopped chives or scallions. Add ½ teaspoon curry powder. Spread on slices of raisin bread, make sandwiches, butter outsides, and broiler-toast both sides. Serve hot.

LADIES' QUICK LUNCHEON

Curried Cream Cheese and Chive Sandwich. Recipe above.

Skewered Fruit Medley. Recipe 203, item 1. Broil alongside sandwiches, turning at the same time. Serve together.

39. TANGY BEAN AND CHEESE SANDWICH

4-6 minutes in preheated broiler

About 5" from heat (3rd shelf in most broilers)

Cut brown bread into thin slices. Spread with baked beans. Top each piece with a thin slice of American cheese and 2 half slices of bacon. Season with cayenne pepper. Broil until bacon is crisp.

SUPPER ON THE PORCH

Tangy Bean and Cheese Sandwich. Recipe above.

Onion Soup, Broiler Style. Recipe 61. Heat in individual ovenware casseroles alongside sandwiches. Serve together.

Crunchy Broiled Peaches. Recipe 199. After removing sandwiches and soup, arrange peaches in pan and broil. Serve separately as dessert.

40. ROLLED GRILLED SANDWICHES

8-10 minutes in preheated broiler

About 5" from heat (3rd shelf in most broilers)

12 to 14 sandwiches

1 large loaf sandwich bread, unsliced
$1/2$ cup melted butter
$1 1/2$ cups filling

Remove crusts from bread and cut lengthwise into 6 or 7 slices. Spread each slice with butter, then with 3 tablespoons of filling. Roll like jelly roll, and wrap in damp napkin until ready to serve. Then butter outsides, slice each roll once crosswise, and broiler-toast both sides. Serve hot. Here are some suggested fillings. Season all of them to taste with salt and pepper.

Pimiento cheese with minced green pepper
Mashed hard-cooked eggs with pickle relish
Chopped parsley with creamed butter
Cream cheese blended well with smoked salmon bits
Ground salami moistened with condensed cream of celery soup
Cottage cheese mixed with minced radishes, cucumbers, and chives
Soft Cheddar cheese and ground or minced olives
Cooked flaked fish mixed with softened butter and parsley flakes
Chopped chicken moistened with mayonnaise

41. SALMON AU GRATIN OPEN SANDWICH

4-6 minutes in preheated broiler

About 5" from heat (3rd shelf in most broilers)

With a fork, mash canned salmon, add minced onion, season to taste with salt and pepper. Broiler-toast bread on one side. Spread untoasted side with butter, prepared mustard, and salmon mixture. Sprinkle generously with grated Parmesan cheese, and broil until cheese melts.

42. SHRIMP SANDWICH

4-6 minutes in preheated broiler

About 5" from heat (3rd shelf in most broilers)

Boil washed shrimp; cool, drain, peel and clean. Mince; add condensed cream of celery soup to spreading consistency. Season with salt and pepper. Broiler-toast bread on one side, pile the shrimp mixture on untoasted side, and return to broiler for a few minutes to heat.

CRUNCHY SUMMER SPREAD

Shrimp Sandwich. Recipe above.
Party Potato Chips. Recipe 16. Watch these. If necessary, remove a minute or two before other food.
Salted Almonds. Recipe 21.
    Broil everything at the same time. Serve together.

43. TUNA MUFFIN

6-8 minutes in preheated broiler

About 5" from heat (3rd shelf in most broilers)

4 servings

1 can (7 ounces) tuna fish, flaked
¼ cup minced gherkins
2 tablespoons minced celery
2 tablespoons minced onion
2 tablespoons mayonnaise
1 teaspoon lemon juice
4 English muffins, split and buttered

(Serve with thick wedges of cheese for a satisfying supper)

Blend tuna, gherkins, celery, onion, mayonnaise, and lemon juice. Broiler-toast muffins until barely touched with brown. Spread tuna mixture on each—add a tomato slice if you like—and return to broiler to heat.

44. THREE-DECKER HAMBURGER

8-10 minutes in preheated broiler

About 5" from heat (3rd shelf in most broilers)

For each sandwich, use 3 slices of white bread, broiler-toasted on one side. Cover untoasted side of 1 slice with thin slice of tomato and 2 half slices of bacon. Cover second slice of bread with very thin hamburger patty. Spread third slice of bread with softened butter. Broil until bacon is crisp and patty is done. Then combine in one sandwich: toast, tomato, bacon on bottom deck; toast, hamburger patty on second deck; buttered bread for top deck. Secure with pick if necessary. Serve with onion slices or with pickles on the side.

45. CHOPPED GIBLET AND BACON OPEN SANDWICH

4-6 minutes in preheated broiler

About 5" from heat (3rd shelf in most broilers)

Cook chicken giblets (heart and gizzard first, liver added in the last few minutes) until tender. Chop fine. Add mayonnaise, salt and pepper to taste. Broiler-toast 2 slices of bread for each sandwich; spread giblet mixture on untoasted side. Cover with bacon slices cut into 1-inch pieces, and broil until bacon is crisp. Serve 2 open sandwiches, garnished with parsley, per person.

46. HEARTY BOLOGNA PUFF

6-10 minutes in preheated broiler

About 5" from heat (3rd shelf in most broilers)

4 servings

8 slices bologna
4 slices bread
1 egg white, beaten stiff
3 tablespoons mayonnaise
1 teaspoon prepared mustard

(A luncheon quickie, good with chilled tomato juice)

Cover each slice of bread with 2 slices of bologna. Combine egg white, mayonnaise, and mustard, and spread over bologna. Broil until tops are puffy and brown. Serve immediately.

47. TOASTED HAM AND SWISS CHEESE

4-6 minutes in preheated broiler

About 5" from heat (3rd shelf in most broilers)

Make a sandwich with 1 slice of Swiss cheese, 1 thin slice of cooked ham spread with prepared mustard, and 2 slices of rye bread. Butter outside of bread, and broiler-toast on both sides until golden brown.

48. TONGUE AND SWISS OPEN SANDWICH

6-10 minutes in preheated broiler

About 5″ from heat (3rd shelf in most broilers)

4 double open sandwiches

1 cup chopped cooked tongue
1 cup Swiss cheese
8 stuffed olives
2 tablespoons mayonnaise
Salt and pepper
8 slices bread

(Prepared mustard on the table will be welcome)

Put tongue, cheese, and olives through the food chopper, using coarse grind. Add mayonnaise, salt and pepper to taste, and mix well. Broiler-toast bread on one side; spread tongue mixture on other side. Heat in broiler until bubbly and serve immediately, garnished with lettuce.

49. CHICKEN SUPPER SPECIAL

5-8 minutes in preheated broiler

About 5" from heat (3rd shelf in most broilers)

4 sandwiches

4 large slices cooked chicken
1 tablespoon shredded pimiento
8 slices bread
2 eggs, slightly beaten
1 cup milk
¼ teaspoon salt

(Hot basil-flavored green beans will make this a super special)

Arrange chicken slices and shredded pimiento on bread slices, and make sandwiches. Mix together eggs, milk, and salt. Dip each sandwich in egg mixture, turning to coat both sides. Broil on well-greased pan until golden brown, turning once.

MIX-MATES

Chicken Supper Special. Recipe above.
Honey-Topped Pineapple Slices. Recipe 201. Broil, without turning, alongside sandwiches. Serve together.

50. LAZY-DAY BAKE FOR YOUNGSTERS

2-4 minutes in preheated broiler

About 5" from heat (3rd shelf in most broilers)

Trim crusts from sliced white bread and, with a rolling pin, roll out bread as thin as possible. Now delight the children with these:

1. Cut fancy shapes with cooky cutters. Brush with melted butter, sprinkle with a mixture of cinnamon and sugar, and broil for a few minutes until sugar browns lightly.

2. Cut out shapes, cover with softened cream cheese, top with chopped nuts. Brown lightly in broiler.

3. Spread rolled-out slices with peanut butter, put a dab of pineapple jam in the center. Roll like jelly roll, pinch ends together to hold, and brown lightly in broiler.

51. BANANA "CAKE" FOR THE SCHOOL CROWD

8-10 minutes in preheated broiler

About 5" from heat (3rd shelf in most broilers)

Cover the inside of a shallow ovenware dish thickly with butter. Then spread with graham cracker crumbs. Fill dish with banana sliced about ½ inch thick, dot top with butter and brown sugar and broil until top is brown.

52. PEANUT BUTTER AND MARSHMALLOW CRUNCH

2-3 minutes in preheated broiler

About 5" from heat (3rd shelf in most broilers)

Spread peanut butter on Holland rusks or zwieback. Top with cut-up marshmallows. Broil until marshmallow browns. Serve with milk as a quick after-school snack.

53. PANCAKE ROLL-UPS

4-6 minutes in preheated broiler

About 5" from heat (3rd shelf in most broilers)

Spread cottage cheese mixed with finely-cut pineapple in the center of freshly-made thin pancakes. Roll up and secure with picks. Brush with melted butter, and broil until butter is bubbly. Serve immediately, with a mixture of cinnamon and sugar.

54. QUICK HOMEMADE CHEESE BLINIS

6-10 minutes in preheated broiler

About 5" from heat (3rd shelf in most broilers)

10 blinis

Cut crusts from 10 slices of white bread and roll as thin as possible with a rolling pin. Lightly mix together ½ pound cottage cheese, 1 egg, 2 tablespoons raisins, and sugar to taste. Place 1 tablespoon of this mixture in center of each slice, pinch ends together to hold, brush outsides with butter. Broil, turning once, until brown. Sprinkle with cinnamon and sugar and serve hot. They "eat well" so allow 2 to 4 for each serving.

55. FROZEN BLINIS

6-10 minutes in preheated broiler

About 5" from heat (3rd shelf in most broilers)

These delectable little mouthfuls are on the market among the frozen foods and are available with various fillings: cheese, berry, cherry, potato. Arrange your favorite selection on a well-buttered pan and broil, turning once, until golden brown. Serve them with sliced strawberries, sour cream, honey, or maple sirup. They *are* good!

56. FROZEN WAFFLES

4-6 minutes in preheated broiler

About 5" from heat (3rd shelf in most broilers)

Put these bought treats under the broiler just long enough to heat, turning once. They are delightful with ice cream from your freezer, or with cinnamon-flavored applesauce which you can heat in an ovenware dish in the broiler along with the waffles.

57. AMERICAN PIZZA

8-12 minutes in preheated broiler

About 5" from heat (3rd shelf in most broilers)

Pull English muffins apart (don't cut) and brush with olive oil. Broiler-toast, open-side up until lightly browned. For each 2 halves, allow ¼ cup cooked drained tomatoes, seasoned to taste with salt, pepper, garlic salt, and a pinch of dried orégano, and enough olive oil to make a smooth consistency. Spread on muffin, cover with a thin slice of Italian mozzarella cheese (or substitute American cheese). Then add any one of the following: anchovy fillet, minced green or black olives, sliced cooked Italian ham, hot red pepper strips, ground beef, or mashed sardine. Broil until cheese is hot and bubbly. Allow at least 2 halves for each serving. It's fun to offer a variety of pizzas and let your guests choose.

58. GRILLED EGGS

2-4 minutes in preheated broiler

About 5" from heat (3rd shelf in most broilers)

2 eggs per serving

Fill a shallow pan with 2 inches of salted water. Bring to boil, then reduce to simmering. Break eggs, slip into water and cook gently, until whites are firm, 2-4 minutes. With a slotted spoon, remove eggs from water, and put 2 in individual ovenware serving dishes. Dot with butter and fine bread crumbs and broil until tops are golden. For a luncheon dish, arrange poached eggs on cooked spinach or asparagus, before broiling.

59. EGGS MORNAY

Follow Recipe 58, but top eggs with white sauce and grated Parmesan cheese instead of butter and bread crumbs. Broil until cheese is golden.

FESTIVE BREAKFAST NOTE

Eggs Mornay. Recipe above.
Anchovy Fingers. Recipe 2. Broil alongside eggs. Serve
     together.

60. WELSH RAREBIT

5-8 minutes in preheated broiler

About 5" from heat (3rd shelf in most broilers)

3 servings

¾ pound American cheese, minced
4 tablespoons milk
1 teaspoon Worcestershire sauce
¼ teaspoon dry mustard
¼ teaspoon paprika
⅛ teaspoon salt
6 slices white bread
Butter

(Substitute tomato sauce for milk for Tomato Rarebit)

Work together all ingredients except bread and butter until mixture is smooth. Broiler-toast bread on one side, butter other side, and spread with cheese mixture. Broil until cheese is bubbly. Serve hot.

BACHELOR'S TREAT

Welsh Rarebit. Recipe above.
Broiled Tomatoes. Recipe 181. Top with French dressing and tarragon.
Nut-stuffed Olives. Recipe 15.
        Broil tomatoes and olives alongside rarebit. Serve together.

61. QUICK HOT SOUPS BROILER STYLE

5-8 minutes in preheated broiler

About 5" from heat (3rd shelf in most broilers)

Use your favorite canned soup. Follow the directions on
the can for adding liquid, pour into individual ovenware
dishes, and heat piping hot in the broiler. Serve with crackers, toast, bread sticks.

Onion Soup. Follow directions on can for adding liquid,
pour into individual ovenware serving dishes, add slices of
French bread, top with grated cheese, and heat in broiler.

ITALIAN-STYLE SUPPER

Minestrone Soup. Recipe above for heating. Buy soup
    canned, top with grated cheese.
Beef Pizza. Recipe 57. Top muffins with ground beef.
    Broil pizza alongside soup. Serve together.

62. PATTY SHELLS WITH MARVELOUS FILLINGS

3-6 minutes in preheated broiler

3"-5" from heat (2nd or 3rd shelf in most broilers)

Patty shells are excellent for parties, fine for luncheons. Make your own, or buy them. Use the tiny ones for hors d'oeuvre, and after filling, put them in the broiler long enough to heat and brown lightly.

Creamed chicken topped with buttered crumbs, garnished with pimiento strips

Saffron-cooked rice, topped with chopped chicken livers moistened with white sauce

Condensed cream of mushroom soup, heated and topped with chopped green peppers

Sliced hard-cooked eggs and cut cooked asparagus, topped with thick sour cream

Creamed shrimp, a dash of white wine, cracker crumbs on top

Cooked sweetbreads and mushrooms, both minced, mixed with white sauce and topped with grated Parmesan cheese

63. BREAKFAST BROIL ON THE TERRACE

8-10 minutes in preheated broiler for first course

About 3" from heat (2nd shelf in most broilers)

4 servings

Grapefruit.   Cut 2 grapefruits into halves. Loosen sections with a sharp knife. Sprinkle each half with 1 tablespoon brown sugar. Broil on rack until lightly browned. Serve. Now lay 12 bacon slices on broiler rack.

Bacon Rolls.   Broil the bacon slices until crisp. Drain on paper towels. Now broiler-toast 4 split and buttered frankfurter rolls. (Watch them, and remove as soon as done.) Fill the rolls with the crisp bacon and serve as sandwiches. Bacon and rolls will be ready in a few minutes.

Hot Coffee Ring.   Buy this, heat in broiler for a few minutes after you remove bacon and rolls and turn off heat. Broiler will stay hot long enough. Try a topping of butter or apricot jam on plain coffee rings. Have lots of hot coffee, made in your electric coffee maker plugged in on another circuit.

beefsteak, veal, and varieties

Beef means beefsteak! And how else can it be served but right from the broiler, proudly covered in its own succulent juices?

Delicious steak is so quick, so easy, so good—and so expensive. Mine is the "don't sear" school, but I have also taken a lesson or two at the "sear" one; so it happens that sometimes I do sear the steak on both sides on the highest shelf, then lower it to the second shelf for slow and even broiling.

How you like it is your business—rare, medium, perhaps well done—but please get a quality cut; otherwise buy hamburgers for this week. They are good too! Or try some of the oddments in this chapter and save up for a choice beefsteak next week.

POINTS TO REMEMBER ABOUT BEEFSTEAK

1. Allow ⅓ to ½ pound for each serving, depending on the amount of bone and fat.

2. Do not pierce meat when turning. Use tongs or insert fork in fat.

3. Brush all meats to be broiled with butter, margarine, or other fat.

4. Allow ¾ to 1 teaspoon salt for each pound of beef.

5. Salt beef after cooking to retain juices, unless it is to be served with a sauce containing the drippings. Then it may be salted ahead.

6. For well-done beef, broil on a shelf lower than the one indicated in these recipes.

7. The best beef cuts for broiled steaks are:

>*Club.* Triangular shape. From rib end of short loin.
>*Porterhouse.* Well marbled. From sirloin end of short loin.
>*Rib.* Cut from rib section.
>*Rump.* Prime rump may be tender enough to broil.
>*Sirloin.* Varies in size and shape. From loin end.
>*Tenderloin* or filet mignon. Tender steaks not widely available.
>*T-bone.* Adjoins club. Has bone shaped like T. From center section of short loin.

8. Do garnish all meat platters. Here are possibilities: strawberries, cherries, chopped chives, parsley, pimientos, radishes, tomatoes, toast strips, and watercress.

64. SIZZLING BROILED STEAK

10-15 minutes in preheated broiler

About 3" from heat (2nd shelf in most broilers)

4 servings

2-pound steak cut 1 inch thick
1 clove of garlic, peeled or cut (optional)
1 tablespoon melted butter, margarine, or oil
1 teaspoon salt
1/4 teaspoon pepper

(Garnish with parsley or watercress for color)

Wipe steak. Slash edge of fat in several places to avoid curling of meat. Rub garlic, if you are using it, on both sides, brush steak with fat and broil on rack until first side is done. Then turn, continue broiling until second side is as you like it; and season it. Serve sizzling steak with pan juices, if any, poured over. Heat the platter on top of the broiler. Follow this time table:

Thickness of cut	*Total broiling time in minutes*		
	RARE	MEDIUM	WELL DONE
1 inch	10-12	12-14	14-16
1½ inches	12-14	14-16	16-20
2 inches	26-28	28-34	34-38

If you like a very brown steak, sear the meat on the highest shelf first; then lower it one or two shelves.

65. ONION-SMOTHERED SIRLOIN

Brown sliced onions lightly in hot fat in a skillet. Spread out on pan below rack. Place steak on rack, then follow directions in Recipe 64. Steak drippings give fine flavor to onions. Arrange these over the steak after you place it on a hot platter.

66. BARBECUED BEEFSTEAK

10-20 minutes in preheated broiler

About 3" from heat (2nd shelf in most broilers)

4 servings

2-pound steak
1 teaspoon dry mustard
1 teaspoon salt
1/4 teaspoon pepper
1 teaspoon sugar
1 teaspoon grated onion
2 tablespoons butter or other fat
Pinch of dried orégano

(Serve with saffron rice or bought tamales for a South-of-the-Border dish)

Broil your favorite cut of steak following the directions in Recipe 64, but do not use a garlic clove on this. While steak cooks, make a paste of the ingredients listed above. When the steak is done, rub the paste into it, and serve broiling hot.

67. SALT-GRILLED STEAK

28-38 minutes in preheated broiler

About 5" from heat (3rd shelf in most broilers)

½ to ¾ pound for each serving

Sirloin steak, cut 2" thick
Salt (about 4 cups)

(A juicy steak which men like)

Wipe steak. Slash edge of fat in several places to prevent
curling. Make a stiff mush of salt with a little water and
spread ½ inch thick on top of steak. Broil for 14 minutes
or until salt layer begins to separate from meat. Lift off
salt with a pancake turner, turn steak, and spread salt mush
on other side. Broil for about 14 minutes more. Then remove salt layer when it has hardened on second side.

Meanwhile, melt lots of butter in an ovenware platter
placed on top of the broiler or set below the broiler pan.
After salt layers are removed, transfer steak to platter.
Broiler-toast 2 slices of French bread for each serving, and
dip them in the butter and juices on the platter. Cut the
steak downward into ½-inch slices, and serve on the succulent slices of bread.

If you use a meat thermometer, insert it in the side of the
steak, face down. When you turn steak, reading side will
be up.

68. PLANKED STEAK FOR TWO

10-15 minutes in preheated broiler

About 3" from heat (2nd shelf in most broilers)

2 servings

1-pound steak cut 1" thick
2 cups mashed potatoes
1 teaspoon salt
¼ teaspoon pepper
Leftover heated vegetable
Butter

(Vegetable ideas: cooked mushroom caps, sliced cooked squash, fried onions)

Broil steak following the directions in Recipe 64. While it broils, heat the plank by resting it on the broiler. Just before the steak is done, spread the plank with butter. Make a border of potatoes around the edges of the plank. Place steak in center, season with salt and pepper, and arrange vegetables between steak and potato border. Or make nests in potatoes by pressing down with spoon and fill with little mounds of hot spinach or string beans, or arrange grilled tomato or eggplant slices. Dot meat and vegetables with butter and return to highest broiling shelf to brown for a few minutes. Serve on plank in a dish of about the same size.

69. LONDON BROIL WITH ONION SAUCE

14-18 minutes in preheated broiler

About 3" from heat (2nd shelf in most broilers)

4 servings

1½-2 pound flank steak
1 clove of garlic, peeled
Strong onion soup (dehydrated type or undiluted condensed)

(Many excellent brands of onion soup are on the market)

Rub steak with cut garlic. Place on rack and broil until done, turning once. Cut diagonal slices about ¼ inch thick. Remove to hot serving platter. Pour on hot onion soup, made according to directions on the package but with only half the recommended amount of liquid. Season at the table if necessary, but the onion soup-sauce probably will be seasoning enough.

TAKE-IT-EASY GRILL

London Broil with Onion Sauce. Recipe above.
Broiled Potato Slices. Recipe 179, but omit garlic. Broil, without turning, alongside flank steak.
Cheese-Filled Mushrooms. Recipe 166. Arrange on rack after turning steak. Broil.

70. BROILED CUBE STEAK

3-5 minutes in preheated broiler

About 3" from heat (2nd shelf in most broilers)

2 servings

4 steaks, ¼ inch thick
2 tablespoons butter, margarine, or other fat

(Cube steaks are usually scored at the market)

Place steaks on broiler rack. Dot with half the butter or other fat, broil, turn, dot with rest of fat. Serve hot, with pan drippings, on buttered toast points or in hot buttered rolls, if you like. Also excellent if spread before broiling with parsley butter, made by working together 2 parts creamed butter and 1 part minced parsley.

FIVE-MINUTE GRILL

Broiled Cube Steak. Recipe above.
Hot Red Caps. Recipe 19.
Buttered Lima Beans. Arrange canned Lima beans in a shallow ovenware dish, top with butter and bread crumbs. Broil mushrooms and Limas alongside steak.

71. CORNED BEEF HASH

12-18 minutes in preheated broiler

About 3" from heat (2nd shelf in most broilers)

4 servings

1 cup chopped cooked corned beef
1½ cups chopped cooked potatoes
3 tablespoons chopped onion
½ teaspoon salt
White sauce

(I never pass this on a restaurant menu, especially with pickle or tomato relish)

Lightly mix together corned beef, potatoes, onion, and salt. Moisten with sauce. Spread evenly in the broiler pan heavily greased with bacon fat. Broil until brown. For a crusty top, raise to highest shelf. Cut into 4 equal sections, remove with pancake turner, and serve. Try canned corned beef hash too. Just slice into 4 parts and broil until lightly browned. Top with cheese strip. Return to broiler to melt cheese, and serve hot.

GARNISH FOR CORNED BEEF HASH

Green Pepper Rings. Cook green pepper rings in a saucepan for a few minutes. Drain, dip in oil, and after turning hash, arrange peppers alongside. Broil until hash is brown.

72. BEEF AND POTATOES BIARRITZ

14-18 minutes in preheated broiler

About 3" from heat (2nd shelf in most broilers)

4 servings

4 cups mashed potatoes
2 tablespoons butter
½ cup light cream
1 teaspoon salt
¼ teaspoon pepper
1 teaspoon chopped parsley
1 teaspoon chopped dill
3 cups cooked beef, cut fine
4 tablespoons grated Parmesan cheese

(A wonderful way to use up leftover beef)

Beat potatoes with butter and cream until smooth. Add seasonings and herbs. Line 4 greased ramekins or shallow casseroles with the potato mixture. Fill each dish with meat. Top with cheese, and broil until brown.

SERVE-TOGETHERS

Beef and Potatoes Biarritz. Recipe above.
Parsley Vienna Loaf. Recipe 24, but spread softened butter and minced parsley between slices. Heat bread on grill, on top of broiler, or for last few minutes place beside casseroles, if there is room.

73. BEEF EN BROCHETTE

4-7 minutes in preheated broiler

About 5" from heat (3rd shelf in most broilers)

For a decorative delight, cut into squares any leftover cooked beef. Let stand in any leftover gravy, or in French dressing for an hour or two in the refrigerator. Then drain, and string on a skewer with alternate wedges of tomato and pearl onions. Heat in the broiler. The onions will be crisp, not soft, and most delicious.

74. BROILED VEAL CHOP WITH ANCHOVIES

8-12 minutes in preheated broiler

About 5" from heat (3rd shelf in most broilers)

4 servings

4 veal chops, cut thin
1 teaspoon salt
2 tablespoons olive oil or other fat
8 flat anchovy fillets

(Sprinkle dried rosemary over chops a few minutes before removing from broiler)

Season chops with salt, and brush with olive oil or other fat. Broil on rack until done, turning once. Just before removing from broiler, top each chop with 2 anchovy fillets. Serve with lemon wedges.

75. VEAL CHOPS MARSALA

8-12 minutes in preheated broiler

About 5" from heat (3rd shelf in most broilers)

4 servings

4 veal chops, cut thin
½ cup Marsala wine
2 tablespoons olive oil
1 teaspoon salt
¼ teaspoon pepper

(Sherry wine may be substituted)

Let chops stand in Marsala for an hour or two. Then drain, reserving the wine. Brush chops with olive oil, season, and broil on rack until done, turning once. Baste several times with the reserved wine. Serve with finely-cut parsley or chopped scallions.

SO-GOOD GRILL

Veal Chops Marsala. Recipe above.
Curried Apple Slices. Recipe 186. Broil alongside chops
　　and at the same time.
Noodles in Tomato Sauce. Recipe 185. After turning
　　chops, arrange noodle casserole on rack, and heat.

76. BROILED SWEETBREADS ON TOAST

8-10 minutes in preheated broiler

About 3" from heat (2nd shelf in most broilers)

4 servings

2 pairs sweetbreads
1 teaspoon salt
4 tablespoons lemon juice
4 slices bacon
4 slices toast

(Make the toast in the broiler)

Soak sweetbreads in cold water to cover for half an hour. Then drain and cover with cold water again, add the salt and lemon juice, and let cook for 15 minutes. Drain, plunge into cold water and, when cool, remove tissues and membrane. Split into 8 large pieces and place on greased broiler rack. Broil until golden, turn, and cover with half a bacon slice. Broil until bacon is crisp. Serve on toast, and garnish with watercress if you like.

COMPANY LUNCHEON

Broiled Sweetbreads on Toast. Recipe above.
Chicken-Filled Mushrooms Amandine. Recipe 168. Broil
   alongside sweetbreads. Serve together.

77. BROILED LIVER AND ORANGE SLICES

4-6 minutes in preheated broiler

About 3" from heat (2nd shelf in most broilers)

4 servings

1 pound calf liver, sliced 1/4-inch thick
2 tablespoons butter, margarine, or other fat
1 teaspoon salt
1/4 teaspoon pepper
2 tablespoons white wine
4 orange slices
1 tablespoon brown sugar

(Variation on the same theme—serve with orange toast)

Wipe the liver. Remove tubes and membranes. Arrange liver on greased broiler rack. Dot with half the fat, and sprinkle with half the salt, pepper, and wine. Place the orange slices on the rack beside the liver. Spread with brown sugar. Broil until liver is done, turning it once, but do not turn orange slices. Serve with chopped chives or parsley, and pan drippings. Remember to heat serving platter in broiler.

78. BROILED LIVER PATTIES

8-10 minutes in preheated broiler

About 3" from heat (2nd shelf in most broilers)

8 patties

1 pound calf or beef liver
1 small onion
1/2 cup fine bread crumbs
1 teaspoon salt
1/4 teaspoon pepper
6 slices bacon
2 tablespoons parsley

(Calf liver is the more delicate, but beef tastes good too)

Put all ingredients through the food chopper, using fine grind. Mix well and shape into patties. (Dip your hands in cold water to make shaping easier.) Broil in a well-greased pan until brown, turning once.

about juicy broiled hamburgers

Properly broiled hamburgers are juicy, satisfying, low-cost and, best of all for a busy woman, they can be done in minutes too. Because they are companionable, you can use them in mixed burger grills with lots of dress-up accompaniments. Try broiling at one time tomato halves or slices, mushrooms, canned pears, peach or pineapple slices, bananas, and cooked or frozen potatoes. Then add a canned green vegetable. You can heat this vegetable too in an ovenware dish under the broiler. Serve a platter meal with bread, buns, or biscuits warmed on top of the broiler, on plates heated under the broiler pan.

Lean broiled hamburgers are also a boon to weight-watchers in the family. Serve them the plain ones, and save

68

the accompaniments, toppings, sauces, and garnishes for the others. See how useful your broiler can be?

POINTS TO REMEMBER ABOUT HAMBURGERS

1. Many beef cuts will do—hanging tenderloin, chuck, flank, neck, heel, round, shoulder—or combinations of these. Or buy good quality ready-ground, or use frozen hamburgers, but lengthen broiling time for these.
2. Allow 1 pound of beef to serve 4, but it need not stretch so far.
3. To keep juices intact, salt and pepper after broiling, unless the drippings will be part of a sauce.
4. Grind beef for hamburgers only once, coarsely, to avoid compactness which toughens them.
5. Handle beef lightly when you shape it. A gentle touch means a juicy hamburger.
6. Line the broiler pan with aluminum foil. It will save washing.
7. If the beef is lean, broil in the pan; if fat, use the rack. Then the fat will drain into the pan.
8. A hamburger is known by many other names: ground beef, patty, beefburger, and meat ball. When other ingredients are added, it sometimes takes its name from the addition: branburger or cheeseburger, for instance. By any name, hamburgers are succulent the broiler way.
9. Sometime brush beef with lemon or lime juice before cooking. It's refreshing!

79. HOW TO BROIL HAMBURGERS

8-12 minutes in preheated broiler

About 3" from heat (2nd shelf in most broilers)

4 servings

1 pound ground beef
1 teaspoon salt
1/4 teaspoon pepper

(If beef is lean, broil on pan: if fat, use rack)

Shape beef into 4 patties about ¾ inch thick. Broil on pan or rack, turning once, until brown. For well-done hamburgers, move to lower shelf after turning. Season when done. Follow this *approximate* time table:

Thickness of patty	Total broiling time in minutes		
	RARE	MEDIUM	WELL DONE
¾ inch	8	10	12
1 inch	12	14	16

80. HAMBURGER TOPPINGS

About 3 minutes before hamburgers are done (Recipe 79)
season them with salt and pepper, and top with any of the
following. Then continue broiling until done.

Dots of butter on 2 slices of dill pickle
Slice of tomato topped with bread crumbs
Slice of Bermuda onion seasoned with prepared mustard
1 teaspoon chopped green pepper mixed with 1 teaspoon grated cheese
Broiled mushroom cap
1 teaspoon sweet pickle relish mixed with 2 teaspoons catsup
Slice minced bacon
Patty of leftover mashed potatoes dotted with parsley butter
1 teaspoon A-1 or Worcestershire sauce mixed with 1 teaspoon prepared horse-radish
2 teaspoons baked beans seasoned with garlic salt
1 teaspoon crumbled Roquefort cheese blended with 1 teaspoon butter or margarine
2 teaspoons red wine mixed with 1 teaspoon melted butter or margarine
1 tablespoon applesauce
2 tablespoons condensed cream of tomato soup

81. HAMBURGER SERVE-ALONGS

To decorate the hamburger plate, select at least one red and one green accompaniment for color—and taste.

RED
Toast points spread with paprika butter
Tomato wedges
Pimiento strips
Shredded canned beets
Potato chips dusted with paprika
Hot red peppers

GREEN
Crisp white crackers spread with parsley butter
Dill pickle slices
Minced chives
Watercress or carrot tops
Green pepper rings
Tiny gherkins

82. STUFFED HAMBURGER SURPRISES

Serve these at your next midnight supper for the crowd. Shape the burgers to fit whatever bun or bread you use. For each stuffed hamburger, make 2 very flat patties. Select one or more of the fillings suggested below. Press edges of patties together to hold filling. Broil and serve on broiler-toasted buttered buns, split buttered English muffins, or on hot waffles.

1 tablespoon minced American cheese
2 small cocktail onions
2 sliced stuffed olives
1 teaspoon chive cheese blended with 1 teaspoon butter
Slices of hard-cooked egg
Slice of tomato sprinkled with basil
2 anchovy fillets rolled around capers
Pineapple wedge sprinkled with ginger
Mixture of 1 teaspoon pickle relish, 1 teaspoon chopped onion, ¼ teaspoon prepared mustard
Mixture of 1 teaspoon chutney and 1 teaspoon chopped nuts

83. BARBECUED BURGER IN BUN

8-12 minutes in preheated broiler

About 3" from heat (2nd shelf in most broilers)

4 servings

1 clove of garlic, peeled and minced
1 minced onion
½ cup salad oil
1 teaspoon salt
½ cup wine vinegar
1 teaspoon prepared mustard
1 tablespoon chili powder
4 tablespoons catsup
1 tablespoon Worcestershire sauce
½ teaspoon orégano
1 bay leaf
1 pound ground beef
4 hamburger buns

(Remove bay leaf before you broil burgers)

In a saucepan, simmer all but the last 2 ingredients for about 10 minutes. Shape beef into 4 patties, place right in broiler pan (to save extra washing), pour sauce over them, and refrigerate for about an hour. Then broil, turning once, until meat is as done as you like. Remove to platter, broiler-toast split hamburger buns for a minute or two, and serve burgers in buns with sauce drippings.

84. SIMPLY ELEGANT CAUCASIAN HAMBURGER

8-12 minutes in preheated broiler

About 3" from heat (2nd shelf in most broilers)

4 servings

1 pound ground beef
¾ teaspoon salt
⅛ teaspoon pepper
½ cup sour cream
1 tablespoon fresh chopped dill
   or ½ teaspoon dill seeds
Paprika

(Sour cream goes surprisingly well with hamburgers)

Shape beef into 4 patties. Broil on rack until done, turning once. Season with salt and pepper. Top each patty with the sour cream mixed with dill seeds, and return to broiler for a minute or two—just long enough to heat cream. Dust with paprika and serve at once.

SUMMER SUPPER

Simply Elegant Caucasian Hamburger. Recipe above.
Broiler Glazed Carrots. Recipe 160.
Potato Blinis. Recipe 55.
> Arrange blinis and carrots alongside hamburgers and turn when necessary. If vegetables are ready before hamburgers, keep them warm on the grill or on ovenware platter in bottom of boiler. Serve together.

85. OPEN BURGER SANDWICH

8-12 minutes in preheated broiler

About 3" from heat (2nd shelf in most broilers)

4 servings

4 hamburger rolls
¾ pound ground beef
½ cup milk
1 teaspoon Worcestershire sauce
1 egg
3 tablespoons grated onion
1 teaspoon catsup
½ teaspoon salt

(Before broiling, place a strip or two of cheese across the top, if you like)

Scoop out centers of hamburger rolls. (There should be about 2 tablespoons of bread from each.) Combine with ground beef and other ingredients and mix lightly. Fill rolls with beef mixture and broil on rack, without turning, until done. Serve hot.

QUICK SNACK

Open Burger Sandwich. Recipe above.
Potato Tidbits. Recipe 8. After turning sandwiches arrange potatoes alongside and continue broiling. Serve together.

86. PATTIES AND PEACHES

8-12 minutes in preheated broiler

About 3" from heat (2nd shelf in most broilers)

4 servings

1 pound ground beef
4 canned peach halves, drained
1 tablespoon sauterne wine
I teaspoon sugar
1/4 teaspoon curry powder
Ground ginger
1 teaspoon salt
1/8 teaspoon pepper
Shredded coconut

(For color, add a green garnish like watercress)

Shape beef into 4 patties and place on broiler rack. Arrange peach halves alongside, hollow side up. Combine wine, sugar, curry powder, and a dash of ginger. Divide mixture equally among peach halves. Broil patties and peaches. Season patties with salt and pepper when done. Serve 1 patty with each peach half, and cover with shredded coconut. (You can brown this too in the broiler for a minute.)

87. HAWAIIAN HAMBURGER DELIGHT

8-12 minutes in preheated broiler

About 3" from heat (2nd shelf in most broilers)

4 servings

1 pound ground beef
1/4 cup soy sauce
4 tablespoons brown sugar
1/2 teaspoon ground ginger
4 slices drained canned pineapple
1 teaspoon salt
1/4 teaspoon pepper

(This has a piquant flavor you will like)

Shape beef into 4 patties and place on broiler rack. Sprinkle with soy sauce. Mix together brown sugar and ginger, spread on pineapple, and arrange on rack beside patties. Broil hamburgers until done as you like them, turning once. Season with salt and pepper.

PRETTY GRILL

Hawaiian Hamburger Delight. Recipe Above.
Vegetable Kebab. Recipe 184. Broil alongside hamburgers. Serve together.
Lemon Toast. Recipe 28. Toast on grill or in broiler for a few moments after removing hamburgers.

88. GLAMOROUS BEEF KEBABS

8-12 minutes in preheated broiler

About 3" from heat (2nd shelf in most broilers)

6 servings

1½ pounds ground beef
1 egg
½ cup fine bread crumbs
1 tablespoon minced parsley
1 tablespoon grated onion
1½ teaspoons salt
¼ teaspoon pepper
12 pearl onions
12 tomato wedges

(Easy eating, pretty as a picture too)

Lightly mix together all ingredients except onions and to-matoes. Shape meat into balls about 2 inches in diameter and string on 6 skewers, 8 inches long, alternating each meat ball with an onion and a tomato wedge. Broil until meat balls are done, turning at least once. Serve hot, garnished with raw green pepper rings perhaps.

INTERESTING IDEA

Glamorous Beef Kebabs. Recipe above.
Waffles. Recipe 56. Broiler-toast waffles after turning
    kebabs. Serve together.

89. HAMBURGER AND EGGPLANT GRILL

13-18 minutes in preheated broiler

About 3" from heat (2nd shelf in most broilers)

4 servings

1 cup French dressing
1 tablespoon grated onion
½ teaspoon dried basil
4 eggplant slices, ¼ inch thick
1 pound ground beef
1 teaspoon salt
¼ teaspoon pepper

(Hamburger drippings add zest to eggplant)

Combine French dressing, onion, and basil, and pour over eggplant slices. Refrigerate for 1 to 2 hours; then place in broiler pan without draining. Broil for about 5 minutes, and turn. Shape beef into 4 patties, broil beside eggplant, turning once, until meat is done. Season hamburgers with salt and pepper, and serve each with an eggplant slice. If you like, top each hamburger in last few minutes with a thick, parsley-sprinkled tomato slice, and broil it too.

bacon, ham, and pork grills

Pork must be cooked well and long, and broiling is not generally advised. But you can really extend the usefulness of your broiler, and have interesting and *easy* meals, if you will plan on complete grills featuring smoked ham slices, and other pork products.

Usually mixed grills, although colorful and luscious, are a little difficult for beginners, since foods which may require different broiling times must be completed at the same time. However, ham slices have an affinity for fruits, and both are easily broiled and served together. So it won't take a *Cordon bleu*, or a juggler, or even a certificate in arithmetic, to follow these recipes.

The broiler is especially useful for big breakfasts. It can hold 10 or 12 bacon slices, many sausage links, and it will warm breakfast buns and plates simultaneously too. Set the broiler on a table that wheels, and serve breakfast this Sunday near a sunny window or beside the fireplace.

90. CANADIAN-STYLE BACON

5-8 minutes in cold broiler

About 5" from heat (3rd shelf in most broilers)

Place slices on rack and broil until lightly brown, turning once. Allow 3 slices for each serving.

91. BROILED PORK SAUSAGES

12-16 minutes in preheated broiler

About 5" from heat (3rd shelf in most broilers)

Place links or patties on broiler rack and broil until brown, turning as often as necessary. Drain on paper towel. Save the drippings for seasoning and frying. Allow 3 or 4 sausages for each serving.

92. BROILED BACON SLICES

3-4 minutes in preheated broiler

6-8 minutes in cold broiler

About 5" from heat (3rd shelf in most broilers)

Place slices on rack, and broil. Turn it once if you like bacon crisp, otherwise turning is not necessary. Drain on paper towel. Save the drippings for seasoning and frying. Allow 2-4 slices for each serving.

93. BROILED READY-TO-EAT MEATS

4-6 minutes in preheated broiler

About 3" from heat (2nd shelf in most broilers)

Many varieties of ready-to-eat meats are on the market. Sliced and broiler-heated, they make quick and appetizing snacks, or are good for a main course. Used as stuffings for tomatoes or mushrooms, and served with broiled fruits, they make attractive grills and have saved the day for many a busy woman. Among ready-to-eat meats are boiled ham, braunschweiger, bologna, tongue, cervelat, cured pork loaf, and salami. There are many others.

94. HOW TO BROIL A HAM SLICE

About 3" from heat (2nd shelf in most broilers)

Slash edges of fat surrounding ham in several places. Lay ham on broiler rack, and broil in preheated broiler until lightly browned on both sides, turning once. Follow this time table:

Thickness of cut	* *Total broiling time*
½-inch uncooked slice	12-15 minutes
¾-inch uncooked slice	15-18 minutes
1-inch uncooked slice	18-22 minutes

* *Reduce time by half for pre-cooked slice*

SUNDAY GRILL FEATURING HAM

Ham Grill. Recipe above.
Crunchy Peaches. Recipe 199.
Garlic Grilled Corn on Cob. Recipe 162.
> After turning ham, broil peaches and corn alongside. If you use pre-cooked ham, broil peaches, corn, and ham together. Turn ham and corn.

95. MUSTARD HAM ON SUCCOTASH

15-18 minutes in preheated broiler

About 3" from heat (2nd shelf in most broilers)

6 servings

2 center slices uncooked smoked ham, ¾ inch thick
3 cups cooked succotash
3 tablespoons brown sugar
2 tablespoons prepared mustard
1 tablespoon oil
1 tablespoon vinegar

*(Combine lima beans and corn with cream for
succotash)*

Slash edges of fat surrounding ham in several places. Spread succotash in broiler pan, put rack over it, and lay ham on top. Broil until lightly brown, turn, and continue broiling. Meanwhile mix other ingredients and spread on top of ham. Continue broiling for about 4 minutes longer. Serve hot.

QUICK MAIN DISH

Mustard Ham on Succotash. Recipe above.
Skewered Fruit Medley. Recipe 203, item 5. Broil alongside ham after turning it. Serve together.

96. HAM-AND-YAM GRILL

20-25 minutes in preheated broiler

About 3" from heat (2nd shelf in most broilers)

Lower to 5" from heat (3rd shelf in most broilers)

4 servings

1 center slice smoked ham 1 inch thick
4 cooked yams or sweet potatoes
2 cups grated American cheese
2 apples, pared and cored
1 tablespoon melted butter or oil
1 tablespoon brown sugar

(For another good dish substitute string beans for yams)

Slash edges of fat surrounding ham in several places to prevent curling. Broil ham in broiler pan for about 12 minutes, turning once. Place halved yams or sweet potatoes on browned ham and sprinkle with cheese. Slice the apples, arrange around ham, and brush with butter or oil. Sprinkle with brown sugar. Move broiler pan to lower shelf and continue broiling until the cheese melts and the apple is golden. (If you use cooked ham, cut broiling time in half and start apples, sweet potatoes, and ham at the same time.)

97. BROILED HAM WITH PINEAPPLE

5-8 minutes in preheated broiler

About 3" from heat (2nd shelf in most broilers)

1 serving

Place cooked ham slice on broiler pan. Lay 2 slices of drained canned pineapple on rack, sprinkle with powdered cloves, and broil until ham and pineapple are lightly browned. Serve ham on top of pineapple.

98. HAM ROLL-UPS WITH BAKED BEANS

6-8 minutes in preheated broiler

About 3" from heat (2nd shelf in most broilers)

1 serving

1 slice cooked ham ⅛ inch thick
Prepared mustard
2 tablespoons hot baked beans

*(Double the broiling time if you use uncooked,
smoked ham)*

Spread ham slice with prepared mustard. Place baked beans on the ham and roll up. Fasten with toothpick and broil on pan until lightly brown, turning once. Serve with canned apricots or peaches.

99. HAM STEAK WITH SAUERKRAUT

5-8 minutes in preheated broiler

About 3" from heat (2nd shelf in most broilers)

2-3 servings

2 cups drained sauerkraut
Ground juniper berries
2 tablespoons shredded pimiento
1 center slice cooked ham, 1/2 inch thick

(Caraway and dill seeds are good with sauerkraut too)

Lay sauerkraut in broiler pan, spreading evenly. Season with juniper berries. Top with pimiento. Place rack over sauerkraut, lay ham slice on top, and lightly brown in the broiler. Turn ham once.

100. PORK, PEPPER, AND PINEAPPLE KEBAB

8-12 minutes in preheated broiler

About 5" from heat (3rd shelf in most broilers)

Cut cooked pork into 1½-inch cubes; cut green peppers into 1½-inch squares; drain canned pineapple chunks. String all of these on a skewer, alternating them. Broil until pork is lightly browned. Baste with pineapple juice, if you like.

101. CHINATOWN SPARERIBS

40-50 minutes in preheated broiler

About 5" from heat (3rd shelf in most broilers)

4 servings

¼ cup honey
½ cup sherry wine
⅛ cup chili sauce
⅛ cup soy sauce
2 garlic cloves, crushed
3 pounds spareribs

(It's the marinade that makes this dish succulent)

Mix together all ingredients except spareribs. Pour the sauce over the spareribs and refrigerate for at least twenty-four hours, turning the ribs occasionally. Drain, but save the marinade. Place spareribs, meaty side up, on broiler pan and broil, turning once, until well-browned. Baste frequently with the marinade. Cut ribs apart (allow about 3 for each serving) and serve well done. Excellent with cooked rice.

frankfurters are festive

Frankfurters are popular with lots of people—the O'Grady's and presidents' ladies, too. And for good reason. They are filling for the family, fun for party fare, always good eating, and excellent budget-balancers as well.

Allow at least 2 franks—or wieners, or hot dogs— for each serving. Serve very hot, with catsup, mustard, horse-radish, olives, and lots of relishes such as chow-chow, chutney, piccalilli, hot peppers. And some say a frankfurter roll too. With broiled wieners at our house, I almost always serve sauerkraut with caraway seeds, or baked beans, or potato salad with dill. Sometimes I serve all three *and* the rolls, *and* the relishes.

Frankfurters are already cooked when you buy them, and need only heating and browning to serve.

102. BROILED FRANKFURTERS

5-8 minutes in preheated broiler

About 3" from heat (2nd shelf in most broilers)

Allow 2 for each serving

Split frankfurters lengthwise, but do not cut completely through. Or leave them whole. Broil on rack until brown, turning once. Serve *hot.*

103. ZESTY FRANK BIRDS

5-8 minutes in preheated broiler

About 3" from heat (2nd shelf in most broilers)

4 servings

8 frankfurters
1 package (3 ounces) chive cream cheese
2 cups hot seasoned mashed potatoes

(Frankfurters get a new look and taste)

Split frankfurters lengthwise, but do not cut completely through. Spread cut side with chive cream cheese; then top with potatoes and dust with paprika. Broil until potatoes are brown. Do not turn or they will lose stuffing. (Remember frankfurters are completely cooked when you buy them.)

104. BARBECUED FRANKFURTERS

5-8 minutes in preheated broiler

About 3" from heat (2nd shelf in most broilers)

4 servings

8 frankfurters
1 small onion, minced
1 clove of garlic, peeled and minced
1/3 cup catsup
3 tablespoons vinegar
1 teaspoon dry mustard
1 teaspoon chili powder
1 teaspoon salt

(For a hotter sauce, use more chili)

Split frankfurters lengthwise, but do not cut completely through. Place in broiler pan, cut side down, and broil until lightly browned. Meanwhile make a sauce by combining all other ingredients in a saucepan. Bring to boiling. Pour hot sauce over frankfurters and serve immediately.

TEENS PORCH PARTY

Barbecued Frankfurters. Recipe above.
Apple Sandwich. Recipe 187. Broil alongside frankfuters.
      Serve together.

105. CORN-STUFFED FRANKFURTERS

6-8 minutes in preheated broiler

About 3" from heat (2nd shelf in most broilers)

4 servings

8 frankfurters
1 tablespoon butter, margarine, or oil
¾ cup soft bread crumbs
½ cup canned corn kernels
1 tablespoon grated onion
5 minced stuffed green olives
Salt
Pepper
8 bacon slices

(And grilled tomatoes for a quick little supper)

Split frankfurters lengthwise but do not cut completely through. In a saucepan, melt butter; stir in all other ingredients except bacon, and let cook about 10 minutes, mixing well but lightly. Spread frankfurters with this mixture. Then wrap a bacon slice around each frankfurter, fasten ends with picks, and broil on rack until bacon is crisp, turning once.

ONE-DISH LUNCHEON

Corn-Stuffed Frankfurters. Recipe above.
Broiled Tomatoes. Recipe 181. Season tomatoes with French dressing. Broil alongside frankfurters.
Paprika Toast. Recipe 28. Pop under broiler after removing frankfurters and tomatoes.

106. FRANKFURTER AND POTATO-ROQUEFORT SALAD

5-8 minutes in preheated broiler

About 3" from heat (2nd shelf in most broilers)

2-4 servings

4 cups cooked potatoes, sliced thin
1 teaspoon salt
1/4 teaspoon pepper
4 minced stuffed green olives
2 tablespoons crumbled Roquefort or blue cheese
3 tablespoons vinegar
4 frankfurters
1 teaspoon prepared mustard

(6 medium potatoes cooked will make 4 cups sliced)

Arrange potatoes in greased broiler pan. Sprinkle over them salt, pepper, olives, cheese, and vinegar. Lay greased broiler rack on top. Place frankfurters, split lengthwise, on rack, spread with mustard, and broil until frankfurters are done, turning once. The drippings will add flavor and dressing to the potato salad below.

LAZY-DAY DISH

Frankfurter and Potato-Roquefort Salad. Recipe above.
Hot Cinnamon Applesauce. Top cooked or canned applesauce, in shallow ovenware dish, with cinnamon. Broil alongside frankfurters. Serve together.

107. FRANKFURTERS AND TOMATOES IN OPEN ROLLS

5-8 minutes in preheated broiler

About 3" from heat (2nd shelf in most broilers)

2 servings

4 frankfurters
4 frankfurter rolls
8 slices tomato
1 teaspoon dried basil
3 tablespoons melted butter, oil, or other fat
1 teaspoon paprika

> *(Melt the butter in a small glass ovenware dish while broiler preheats)*

Split frankfurters lengthwise, but do not cut completely through. Split rolls and place cut-side up on broiler rack. Cover each completely with slices of tomato. Sprinkle with basil. Place frankfurters on tomatoes. Brush with butter or other fat. Broil until brown, turning frankfurters if you wish. (Turning is not necessary, since frankfurters are cooked when you buy them.)

108. TROPICAL FRANKFURTERS ON SKEWERS

5-8 minutes in preheated broiler

About 3" from heat (2nd shelf in most broilers)

4 servings

8 frankfurters
1/4 cup soy sauce
1/2 cup pineapple juice
2 tablespoons lemon juice
2 tablespoons prepared mustard
36 pineapple chunks (14-ounce can)

(Enough to fill 8 skewers 8 inches long)

Cut frankfurters into inch-thick slices. Combine soy sauce, pineapple and lemon juice, and mustard. Let franks stand in this mixture for an hour or two in the refrigerator. Then drain and string on skewers, alternating slices of franks with chunks of pineapple. Use an end piece of frankfurter first and last. Broil until frankfurters are brown, turning skewers several times. Serve skewers in paper napkins to make this a finger food.

FINGER FOOD

Tropical Frankfurters on Skewers. Recipe above.
Apricot Sandwich Treat. Recipe 30. Make 2 sandwiches
   to serve 4. Broil alongside frankfurters. Cut each
   sandwich into 4 triangles and serve.

109. CHEESE-STUFFED FRANKFURTERS

5-8 minutes in preheated broiler

About 3" from heat (2nd shelf in most broilers)

2 servings

4 frankfurters
4 slices sharp Cheddar cheese
4 slices bacon

(Serve with sauerkraut heated under the broiler rack)

Split frankfurters lengthwise, but do not cut completely through. Lay a slice of cheese, folded several times, in each one. Wrap a slice of bacon around each frankfurter, fasten ends with picks, and broil on rack until bacon is done, turning once.

GAME-ROOM SPREAD

Cheese-Stuffed Frankfurters. Recipe above.
Curried Apple Slices. Recipe 186. Broil alongside frankfurters. Serve together.

110. WIENER BINGE FOR TEEN-AGERS

5-8 minutes in preheated broiler

About 3" from heat (2nd shelf in most broilers)

8 servings

6 cups (3 No. 303 cans) baked beans
1/4 cup catsup
2 tablespoons sweet pickle relish
1 tablespoon prepared mustard
8 frankfurters

(A pinch or two of orégano adds zest to beans)

Lightly mix beans, catsup, relish, and mustard, and spread in greased broiler pan or in shallow ovenware casserole. Slash franks diagonally every 2 inches, but do not cut through. Place frankfurters on top of bean mixture and cook until brown, turning frankfurters once if desired. (This is not necessary, however.) Serve on split buttered rolls which have been heated on top of broiler. Chopped onions are good with this.

lamb in the broiler

Since most lamb requires long slow cooking, for which the broiler is not suited, this chapter has fewer recipes than the others. However, more recipes are given in Part II, pages 184 to 187. Even if you do not have a rotisserie those recipes can be useful. For the spit, substitute skewers, arrange them in the broiler pan, and turn by hand.

Mutton can be used instead of lamb, but as it is older, it is also tougher, so increase the broiling time slightly. Lamb or mutton may be served well done or medium, piping hot or refrigerator cool, but it must never be served lukewarm. Lukewarm lamb is tasteless. Remember also to warm the serving plates—place them in the bottom of the broiler for the last few minutes of cooking time.

III. HOW TO BROIL LAMB CHOPS

About 3" from heat (2nd shelf in most broilers)

Buy rib, loin, or shoulder lamb chops. Allow 1 or 2 chops for each serving. Trim excess fat, slash edges in several places to prevent curling. Season with salt and pepper, and, if you like, brush with garlic and sprinkle with dried herbs. Basil, thyme, rosemary, marjoram are popular choices. Place chops on greased broiler rack, and broil in preheated broiler until browned on both sides, turning once with tongs. Follow this approximate table, allowing maximum time for well-done chops.

Thickness of chop	Total broiling time
½ inch	7-10
¾ inch	9-11
1 inch	11-15
1½ inch	16-19
*2 inches	19-24

* Lower to 5 inches from heat after turning

LAMB GO-TOGETHERS

Hot Sauerkraut
Frozen Fried Potatoes
Stuffed Dill Tomatoes
Broiler Glazed Carrots
Green Pepper Rings

112. LAMB CHOP AND FRUIT GRILL

14-18 minutes in preheated broiler

About 3" from heat (2nd shelf in most broilers)

4 servings

4 thick shoulder lamb chops
Salt
Pepper
Rosemary
4 canned pineapple slices, drained
4 canned peach halves, drained
4 tablespoons mayonnaise
4 bananas, peeled
Brown sugar

(A colorful and appealing grill)

Trim excess fat from chops and slash edges in several places to prevent curling. Season with salt and pepper and a pinch of rosemary. Arrange pineapple slices in broiler pan, cover with rack, and put chops on rack. Broil until brown on one side, and turn. Place peach halves, with 1 tablespoon of mayonnaise in each, on rack. Sprinkle bananas with brown sugar, put on rack. Continue broiling until chops are brown and done as you like them. Arrange a chop with fruit around it for each serving.

LOW-CALORY MAIN DISH

Lamb Chop and Fruit Grill. Recipe above. Omit mayonnaise on peaches and give merest hint of sugar to bananas.

113. STUFFED LAMB CHOPS

14-18 minutes in preheated broiler

About 3" from heat (2nd shelf in most broilers)

4 servings

4 loin lamb chops, about 1¼ inches thick
¼ cup fine bread crumbs
3 tablespoons applesauce
2 tablespoons chopped celery
Salt and pepper
Chopped basil leaves

(Turn chops with tongs or with fork inserted in fat)

Trim excess fat from chops, and slash edges in several places to prevent curling. Cut a pocket in the side of each chop. Make stuffing by mixing crumbs, applesauce, celery, salt and pepper to taste. Stuff pocket and fasten with picks. Sprinkle chops with basil leaves, and broil on greased rack until brown and done as you like them, turning once. Remove picks and serve.

114. BROILED LAMB STEAK

14-18 minutes in preheated broiler

About 3" from heat (2nd shelf in most broilers)

4 servings

1 to 1½ pounds lamb steak, cut from leg
Salt
Pepper
2 tablespoons butter
1 tablespoon marjoram

(Serve applesauce topped with mint jelly)

Broil steaks on greased broiler rack until almost done, turning once. Season both sides with salt and pepper. Cream together butter and marjoram, spread on lamb steak, and continue broiling for a minute or two longer.

DRESSED-UP CLUB PLATE

Broiled Lamb Steak. Recipe above.
Eggplant Patties. Recipe 163. Broil alongside lamb, turning at the same time.
Anchovy Fingers. Recipe 2. Broiler-toast for a few minutes after removing lamb and patties.

115. LAMB PATTIES

12-16 minutes in preheated broiler

About 3" from heat (2nd shelf in most broilers)

6 patties

1 pound ground raw lamb
1 tablespoon grated onion
1 teaspoon salt
1/8 teaspoon pepper
Dash of ground mace (optional)
2 tablespoons oil

(Heat toast, bread, or biscuits in bottom of broiler)

Lightly combine all ingredients, except oil, and shape into 6 patties. Place on greased broiler rack, brush with oil, and broil until brown, turning once. Serve with parsley toast or on hot buttered biscuits.

FIFTEEN-MINUTE GRILL

Lamb Patties. Recipe above.
Peach Tartare. Recipe 199. Broil alongside patties.
Dill-Broiled Potato Slices. Recipe 179, but substitute dill seasoning for garlic. Broil alongside patties.

116. HEAVENLY LAMB IN PATTY SHELLS

10-12 minutes in preheated broiler

About 5" from heat (3rd shelf in most broilers)

4 servings

1½ cups cooked lamb
2 tablespoons finely chopped onion
2 tablespoons chopped green pepper
2 tablespoons butter, oil, or other fat
2 tablespoons minced pimiento
½ cup diced cooked potatoes
1 teaspoon salt
⅛ teaspoon pepper
1 cup medium white sauce
4 patty shells

(Or use individual ramekins in place of patty shells)

Cut the lamb fine but do not grind. Brown the onions and green pepper in fat until they are soft. Then combine all other ingredients and spoon into the patty shells. Broil on rack until top is nicely browned. For extra deliciousness, sprinkle grated cheese over the hash before broiling.

117. LAMB SHORTCAKE

Follow Recipe 116, but broil the hash on split-and-buttered baking powder biscuits instead of in patty shells.

118. SWEET LAMB KEBAB

6-10 minutes in preheated broiler

About 3" from heat (2nd shelf in most broilers)

Allow 2 skewers for each serving

Leftover cooked lamb
Cooked apricots
Pineapple chunks
Green maraschino cherries (optional)

(A perfect finish for a leg of lamb)

Cut leftover lamb into 1½-inch squares. On 6-inch skewers, string alternately apricots, lamb squares, and pineapple chunks. If you wish, add a green maraschino cherry for color. Let skewers stand in pineapple sirup for about an hour. Then drain and broil long enough to heat lamb and lightly brown fruit. Serve hot.

QUICK-SERVING IDEA

Sweet Lamb Kebab. Recipe above.

Cinnamon Frankfurter Rolls. Split (not all the way through), and butter rolls. Sprinkle with cinnamon. Broiler-toast alongside kebabs for 2 or 3 minutes. Serve kebabs in rolls.

119. GRILLED LAMB KIDNEYS

9-12 minutes in preheated broiler

About 3" from heat (2nd shelf in most broilers)

4 servings

8 lamb kidneys
1/4 cup French dressing
Salt and pepper

> *(Grill bacon when you turn kidneys and serve together)*

Carefully wash and split kidneys, remove fat and tubes. Let stand in French dressing for about an hour. Then drain, season with salt and pepper, and broil on pan, turning once, until done. Serve on hot buttered garlic toast made in the broiler.

broiled chicken, turkey, and duck

Crunchy chicken in the broiler is traditional, but recently a small turkey has come on the market that is bred for broiling. At its best—and its best is very good indeed—poultry should be crackling-crisp outside, tender and juicy inside. To achieve this state of culinary grace, slow broiling is essential. You will note that in these recipes the poultry is cooked about 5 inches from the heating unit. If you wish to slow the process, so that an even crisper bird will result, lower the pan to the shelf below. To test doneness, cut into the leg joint where no pink should appear.

Young plump birds are best for broiling. Broiler-fryers weighing 3½ pounds or less will be most tender. Turkeys should weigh 6 or 7 pounds. Ducklings weighing 5 to 6 pounds are fine for broiling.

POINTS TO REMEMBER ABOUT CHICKEN, TURKEY, AND DUCK

Poultry is usually sold in any of the following ways:

New York or Market Dressed: Feathers are removed, but head and feet are still on. If requested, your butcher will draw the bird *after* weighing it.

Drawn or Table-ready: Feathers, head, feet, and entrails are removed. Before refrigerating the bird, give a final clean-up to insides. Be sure to remove the oil sac. Remove any remaining pinfeathers with tweezers. Now the bird is ready to cook.

In Parts: You can buy legs, breast, wings, or giblets, instead of or in addition to a whole bird.

Frozen Eviscerated: Ready to cook, drawn, cleaned, and packaged quick-frozen, or stored in the market on ice. Defrost frozen chicken before broiling.

How much to allow for each serving:
Chicken and Turkey
    Dressed: ¾ to 1 pound
    Ready to Cook: ⅔ to ¾ pound
Duck
    Dressed: 1¼ pounds
    Ready to Cook: ¾ to 1 pound

120. HOW TO BROIL CHICKEN TO PERFECTION

30-40 minutes in preheated broiler

About 5" from heat (3rd shelf in most broilers)

2 servings

1 split broiler-fryer (1½ to 2 pounds ready to cook)
½ lemon
Salt
Pepper
Melted butter, chicken fat, or oil

(You'll always enjoy this easy and delicious favorite)

Clean, wash, dry the chicken. Rub all over with lemon. Brush with butter or other fat. Place in broiler *pan*—juices keep chicken moist—skin-side down. Sprinkle with salt and pepper. Broil until brown and tender, turning once. If convenient, baste every 15 minutes with butter or fat. Be sure there is no pink meat left near the bone before you serve. (Cut into the leg joint to see.) Serve with pan drippings.

121. CHICKEN VERMOUTH

Broil as directed in Recipe 120, but baste with a mixture of equal parts of Italian vermouth and olive oil. No other seasonings will be needed.

122. BROILER ON A PLANK FOR ONE

30-40 minutes in preheated broiler

About 5" from heat (3rd shelf in most broilers)

1 serving

½ broiler-fryer (about 1 pound ready to cook)
Salt and pepper
4 tablespoons butter, margarine, or oil
2 teaspoons chopped green pepper
1 teaspoon grated onion
2 teaspoons sliced mushrooms
½ clove minced garlic
1 teaspoon chopped parsley
1 teaspoon lemon juice
1 cup well-seasoned mashed potatoes
Watercress for garnish

(Your broiler can hold two planks so double this)

Clean, wash, dry the chicken. Sprinkle with salt and pepper. Dot with 1 tablespoon fat, place in broiler pan, skin-side down. Broil until almost done, turning once. Meanwhile cream remaining 3 tablespoons butter; add pepper, onion, mushrooms, garlic, parsley, and lemon juice. Heat a large plank on the broiler, then brush it with butter. Spoon a border of mashed potatoes around the edge of the plank or force through a pastry tube to make a pretty design. Lay the almost-done chicken in the middle of the plank, skin-side up. Spread the butter-mushroom mixture over chicken, and return the plank to the broiler to brown the potatoes. To serve, put the plank on a hot platter of about the same size. Garnish with watercress.

123. RAISIN-STUFFED CHICKEN INDIENNE

30-40 minutes in preheated broiler

About 5" from heat (3rd shelf in most broilers)

4 servings

1 quartered broiler-fryer (2½ to 3 pounds ready to cook)
Salt and pepper
½ cup seedless raisins
3 tablespoons peanut butter
3 tablespoons butter, oil, or margarine
2 teaspoons curry powder
Juice 1 lemon

> *(Serve with chopped bacon, chutney, broiled bananas, hot peppers, shredded coconut, cocktail onions, any or all)*

Clean, wash, and dry chicken and place in broiler pan. Sprinkle with salt and pepper. Blend raisins, peanut butter, fat, curry, and lemon juice. Carefully lift edges of skin of chicken and lightly stuff the mixture under the skin. Broil until brown and tender, turning once.

CAREER GIRLS PARTY

Raisin-Stuffed Chicken Indienne. Recipe above.
Broiled Canned Apricots. Recipe 191. Broil alongside chicken several minutes before it is done. Serve together.

124. BARBECUED BROILER

30-40 minutes in preheated broiler

About 5" from heat (3rd shelf in most broilers)

4 servings

2 split broiler-fryers (each 1½ to 2 pounds ready to cook)
¼ cup melted butter or margarine
Juice 1 lemon
2 tablespoons Worcestershire sauce
2 tablespoons vinegar
2 tablespoons catsup
1 teaspoon Tabasco sauce
2 teaspoons salt

(If you like, add a mashed clove of garlic to the sauce)

Clean, wash, and dry chickens. Place in broiler pan, skin-side down. In a saucepan, combine all the other ingredients and bring to a boil. Then brush mixture over chickens. Broil, basting and turning several times until dark red-brown.

125. CHINESE HONEYED CHICKEN

Combine 2 tablespoons soy sauce, 4 tablespoons honey, and 1 egg yolk. Clean, wash, and dry split broiler-fryer. Brush mixture over chicken. Broil as directed in Recipe 120.

126. COUNTRY-STYLE CHICKEN

30-40 minutes in preheated broiler

About 2″ and 5″ from heat (1st and 3rd shelf in most broilers)

4 servings

1 disjointed broiler-fryer (2½ to 3 pounds ready to cook)
2 cups milk
1 teaspoon salt
⅛ teaspoon pepper
1 tablespoon flour
¼ cup melted butter or margarine
Dash of paprika

Lots of city folk love this dish

Wash and dry the chicken. Soak it for several hours in cold milk seasoned with salt and pepper. Drain, reserving the milk. Dust chicken with flour and dip in melted butter. Brown in broiler pan about 2 inches from heat, then lower to 5 inches from heat. Continue broiling, turning once. Add paprika to milk in which chicken was soaked, and cook in saucepan for about 10 minutes over low heat. A few minutes before chicken is done, pour the milk over the chicken, and continue broiling until done.

127. PARSLEY CHICKEN WITH GIBLET GRAVY

30-40 minutes in preheated broiler

About 5" from heat (3rd shelf in most broilers)

2 servings

2 split broiler-fryers (each 1½ to 2 pounds ready to cook)
4 tablespoons oil
6 tablespoons sherry wine
2 tablespoons chopped fresh parsley
Giblets
1 tablespoon butter or margarine
1 teaspoon flour

(Use the giblet gravy for other chicken recipes too)

Clean, wash, and dry chicken. Mix oil, wine, and parsley and pour over chicken. Refrigerate for several hours. Place chicken in broiler pan skin-side down. Pour over it the marinade in which it was soaked. Broil, turning once, until chicken is brown. Serve with giblet gravy.

GIBLET GRAVY

Clean the heart, gizzard, and liver. Simmer heart and gizzard in covered saucepan in 1 cup salted water until almost tender. Then add liver and continue cooking for a few minutes more. Cool giblets, chop, and put back in liquid in which cooked. After the chicken is broiled, add the pan drippings to the liquid. Thicken slightly with butter or margarine blended with flour; season to taste, spoon over chicken, and serve hot.

128. CHICKEN ASPARAGUS

12-15 minutes in preheated broiler

About 5" from heat (3rd shelf in most broilers)

4 servings

12 cooked asparagus tips
2 tablespoons butter or margarine
2 cups cooked chicken
1 cup medium white sauce
1 teaspoon salt
¼ teaspoon pepper
4 tablespoons buttered bread crumbs

(Or substitute cooked drained spinach for asparagus)

Arrange asparagus in greased individual shallow ovenware dishes and dot with butter or margarine. Lightly mix chicken with white sauce (made partly with milk, partly with vegetable liquid), salt and pepper, and pour over asparagus. Top each dish with bread crumbs. Broil until lightly brown. So good for luncheon!

LUNCHEON TREAT

Chicken Asparagus. Recipe above.
Broiled Kadota Figs. Recipe 195.
Lemon Toast. Recipe 28.
    Broil figs and toast alongside chicken for the last few minutes.

129. CHICKEN TETRAZZINI

12-18 minutes in preheated broiler

About 5" from heat (3rd shelf in most broilers)

4 servings

3 tablespoons chicken fat, butter, or margarine
1/3 cup diced green pepper
1/3 cup diced onion
1/3 cup chopped canned shredded pimientos
1/2 cup canned sliced mushrooms
1 teaspoon salt
1/4 teaspoon pepper
2 cups cooked chicken
2 cups cooked spaghetti
2 tablespoons grated Parmesan cheese

(Or you can use undiluted condensed cream of mush-room soup to top chicken before broiling)

Heat fat in saucepan, and cook green pepper and onion until soft. Add drained pimientos, drained mushrooms (save the liquid), salt, pepper, and chicken. Heat for a few minutes. Spread spaghetti in greased broiler pan or in individual shallow ovenware dishes, and top with chicken mixture. Pour the mushroom liquid over all and sprinkle with cheese. Broil until brown and bubbly.

130. CHICKEN GIBLETS

8-12 minutes in preheated broiler

About 5" from heat (3rd shelf in most broilers)

2 servings

Cooked giblets (heart, gizzard, liver)
1/2 small peeled onion
1 cup condensed cream of chicken soup
1 cup seasoned mashed potatoes
1 cup cooked spinach
1 tablespoon grated cheese

(Economy and flavor team up)

Put chicken giblets and onion through the food chopper using fine grind. Cover with soup and heat in a saucepan. Line the sides of shallow individual greased ovenware dishes with mashed potatoes. Spread cooked spinach over the bottom. Pour giblet mixture over spinach, sprinkle with cheese, and broil until brown.

ECONOMY SUPPER

Chicken Giblets. Recipe above.

Mushroom Mounds. Recipe 7. A few minutes before giblets are done, arrange mushrooms on rack alongside giblets.

Pineapple-Filled Broiled Grapefruit. Recipe 197. Broil for about 8 minutes after removing giblets and mounds. Serve as dessert.

131. CHICKEN LIVER PLATTER

10-15 minutes in preheated broiler

About 5" from heat (3rd shelf in most broilers)

3-4 servings

12 chicken livers
Juice 1 lemon
3 tablespoons melted butter or margarine
3 tablespoons white wine
2 tablespoons minced parsley
1 teaspoon salt
1/4 teaspoon pepper
6 to 8 tomato halves or thick slices
4 small onions, sliced

(Serve on hot rice mixed with parsley)

Let livers stand in lemon juice, butter or margarine, wine, parsley, salt, and pepper for several hours in the refrigerator. Drain, reserving the marinade. Arrange the livers on the broiler rack, and place tomatoes and onions alongside. Broil until livers are brown, turn, add remaining marinade, turn tomatoes, and onions, and continue broiling until done.

EASY-TO-FIX GRILL

Chicken Liver Platter. Recipe above.
Garlic French Bread. Recipe 24. Toast bread alongside
　　livers for a few minutes before they are done.
　　Serve together.

132. BROILED DUCKLING

40-60 minutes in preheated broiler

About 5" from heat (3rd shelf in most broilers)

4-5 servings

1 quartered duckling (4 to 4½ pounds ready to cook)
1 clove of garlic
Salt and pepper
Powdered ginger
1 cup orange juice

(Or baste the duckling with apple brandy)

Clean, wash, and dry duckling. Rub inside and out with cut garlic. Sprinkle with salt, pepper, and ginger. Broil, skin-side up, on broiler rack, turning twice, until brown. Baste with orange juice every 10 to 15 minutes. Serve with mashed sweet potatoes heaped in orange shells.

133. BROILED SQUABS

20-30 minutes in preheated broiler

About 5" from heat (3rd shelf in most broilers)

Have squabs cleaned, drawn and split down the back. Brush with sauterne wine, and broil until brown, turning once. Baste frequently with butter. Serve with chopped parsley and drippings sprinkled over them. Allow 1 squab for each serving. This is a festive dish.

134. BROILED YOUNG TURKEY

40-60 minutes in preheated broiler

About 5" from heat (3rd shelf in most broilers)

Buy a disjointed junior turkey, allowing about ¾ pound
for each serving. Follow Recipe 120. Test drumstick (hold
in a paper towel) between thumb and forefinger, to be
sure it is tender before serving.

grilled fish and shellfish

Fish is the food of gourmets. Served plain or served saucy, delicately bathed in herb butter or tipsy with wine, this universal favorite is altogether-delightful eating.

And, as if flavor were not sufficient reason for its culinary being, fish and shellfish are economical, probably as nutritive as a box of vitamin pills, easily digested, and quickly cooked. A thriving frozen-foods industry has made fish—all varieties in all seasons—as available as your nearest grocery.

Fish are meant to be broiled. Good restaurateurs know it for that is their favorite style of cooking when fish is on the menu. Choose the varieties that never counted calories (a partial list follows) and enjoy gastronomic treats at many a meal.

POINTS TO REMEMBER ABOUT FISH AND SHELLFISH

Fish are available in any of the following ways:

Whole or "Round": Complete with all accessories—head and tail, entrails and fins—exactly as caught. Allow ½ to ¾ pound for each serving

Drawn: Scales and entrails removed. Allow ½ to ¾ pound for each serving

Dressed: Scales, entrails, head, tail, fins removed. Allow ½ pound for each serving

Steaks: Boneless slices, cut crosswise. Allow ⅓ pound for each serving

Fillets: Boneless slices, cut lengthwise. Allow ⅓ pound for each serving

Kinds to Broil: Fat fish broil best. Any of the following—fresh, canned, or quick-frozen—can be successfully grilled. This is *part* of the story; so much is left unsaid! Don't be timid about experiments with other varieties.

Fish		
barracuda	mullet	tuna
bass	perch	weakfish
bluefish	pike	whitefish
butterfish	pompano	
catfish	salmon	
cod	scrod	*Shellfish*
flounder	shad	clams
haddock	sheepshead	crabs
hake	smelt	frogs legs
halibut	sole	lobster
herring	sturgeon	oysters
mackerel	swordfish	scallops
	trout	shrimps

135. HOW TO BROIL WHOLE OR SPLIT FISH

8-12 minutes in preheated broiler

About 3" from heat (2nd shelf in most broilers)

Broil small fish whole. Cut large fish into steaks ½- to 1-inch thick, or split them down the back and open flat. Wash and dry fish. To heighten flavor, sprinkle with lemon juice. Dot with butter, margarine, or other fat. Broil in greased broiler pan, not on rack, until golden. Turn, dot with more fat, and continue broiling until done. Fish is cooked when flesh is opaque and flakes easily if tested with a fork. Season with salt and pepper, and serve with pan drippings, and melted butter. Add herbs to butter, or a dash of wine.

136. HOW TO BROIL FISH STEAKS

12-15 minutes in preheated broiler

3"-5" from heat (2nd or 3rd shelf in most broilers)

Wash and dry steaks. Sprinkle with lemon juice, about 1 tablespoon for each pound. Dot with butter, margarine, or other fat. Broil in greased broiler pan until done, turning once with spatula. Dot with fat after turning. Season and serve hot.

137. HOW TO BROIL FISH FILLETS

7-10 minutes in preheated broiler

About 3" from heat (2nd shelf in most broilers)

Sprinkle fillets with lemon juice. Dot with butter, margarine, or other fat. Broil in greased broiler pan, without turning, until done. Season and serve.

138. HOW TO BROWN FISH

Move broiler pan to highest shelf for the last few minutes of broiling. Or add paprika before or during broiling. Or dip fish in egg and bread crumbs or flour before broiling. Or baste frequently with butter or margarine while broiling.

139. PLANKED BROILED FISH

Any fish may be planked. Place the almost-cooked fish—whole, fillets, or steaks—in the center of a hot greased plank. (Heat plank in the broiler while the fish cooks.) Border the plank with seasoned mashed potatoes, brush with melted butter or egg yolk. Put the plank back into the broiler until the fish is done and the potatoes are brown. To be really elegant, squeeze the potatoes through a pastry tube. For variety, before broiling, make nests in the mashed potatoes with the back of a spoon. Fill the nests with drained peas, and dot with butter, before broiling.

140. CELERY-STUFFED BLUEFISH

8-12 minutes in preheated broiler

About 3" from heat (2nd shelf in most broilers)

4 servings

2 bluefish (1½ pounds each) dressed and split
2 tablespoons lemon juice
Salt
Pepper

*(Garnish ideas: thin slices of cucumber and beet
        mounds)*

Sprinkle fish with lemon juice and refrigerate for two
hours. Pile the stuffing in the broiler pan and fit the fish
over it, skin-side up. Broil until flesh is flaky when tested
with a fork, and opaque. Season and serve.

CELERY STUFFING

¾ cup minced celery
2 tablespoons melted butter
½ cup crumbled soda crackers, moistened
½ teaspoon salt
⅛ teaspoon pepper
1 tablespoon minced parsley

In a saucepan, cook celery in butter until tender. Blend in
other ingredients, and heat. "Stuff" fish as directed above.

141. FLOUNDER FILLETS IN WINE SAUCE

7-10 minutes in preheated broiler

About 3" from heat (2nd shelf in most broilers)

2-3 servings

1 pound flounder fillets
3 tablespoons butter or margarine
2 tablespoons sauterne wine
2 tablespoons fine bread crumbs
Salt
Pepper

(Sprinkle with a teaspoon of chopped chives
if you like)

Place fillets in greased broiler pan. Dot with butter or margarine. Broil, basting several times with the sauterne. Just before fish is done, sprinkle with bread crumbs, salt, and pepper. Broil a minute longer to brown crumbs. Serve with lemon wedges.

TEN-MINUTE GRILL

Flounder Fillets in Wine Sauce. Recipe above.
Potato Cakes. Recipe 176. Broil alongside fish.
Broiled Tomatoes. Recipe 181. Top with paper-thin
    onion slices and prepared mustard.

142. ROLLED AND STUFFED FLOUNDER FILLETS

7-10 minutes in preheated broiler

About 3" from heat (2nd shelf in most broilers)

3 servings

1 pound flounder fillets
2 cooked carrots
3 tablespoons soft butter or margarine
1 tablespoon minced parsley
½ teaspoon salt
Dash of pepper

(Or roll fillets around whole cooked carrots)

Place flounder fillets in broiler pan. With a fork, mash together carrots, butter or margarine, parsley, salt and pepper. Spread mixture over each fillet. Roll up and fasten with a toothpick. Broil, turning once, until fish is golden. Serve with lemon wedges dipped in paprika.

FRIDAY MAIN DISH

Rolled and Stuffed Flounder Fillets. Recipe above.
Lima Beans with Cheese. Recipe 185. Broil alongside fish.

143. HADDOCK FILLETS IN HERB BUTTER

7-10 minutes in preheated broiler

About 3" from heat (2nd shelf in most broilers)

4 servings

1½ pounds haddock fillets
2 tablespoons lemon juice
4 tablespoons butter
½ teaspoon dried dill
½ teaspoon minced parsley
½ teaspoon salt
¼ teaspoon pepper

(Just as good with flounder or cod fillets)

Place fillets in greased broiler pan. Sprinkle with lemon juice. Cream together butter, dill, parsley, salt, and pepper. Spread half the mixture over fillets and broil until fish is almost done, without turning. Spread rest of mixture over fillets and broil for a minute or two until fish is done and the butter is melted. Serve.

SEASHORE SUPPER

Haddock Fillets in Herb Butter. Recipe above.
Potato Jamboree. Recipe 178. Broil alongside fish.
Parsley Rye Toast. Recipe 28. Toast in broiler for a few
    minutes after removing fish and potatoes.

144. GOURMET HALIBUT GRILL

12-15 minutes in preheated broiler

3"-5" from heat (2nd or 3rd shelf in most broilers)

4 servings

4 halibut steaks 1'' thick (1½ pounds)
4 tablespoons butter
1 medium-sized tomato, chopped fine
1 medium-sized onion, chopped fine
2 tablespoons minced parsley
4 tablespoons sliced mushrooms
¼ cup sauterne wine
1 teaspoon salt
⅛ teaspoon pepper

(The seasonings have character . . . good too with
bass, haddock, cod)

Place steaks in greased broiler pan. Dot with 2 tablespoons butter. Mix together all other ingredients. Spread half the mixture over steaks. Broil until upper half of flesh is opaque. Turn and dot with remaining butter. Spread rest of tomato mixture and continue broiling until done.

COMPANY TREAT

Gourmet Halibut Grill. Recipe above.

Buttered Potato Balls. Drain small canned potato balls, brush with butter, season with salt and paprika, and broil alongside fish, turning once.

Roquefort Broiled Pears. Recipe 200. Broil alongside fish and potato balls. Serve together.

145. LEMON-BROILED MACKEREL

8-12 minutes in preheated broiler

About 3" from heat (2nd shelf in most broilers)

4 servings

3-pound mackerel, dressed and split
Juice 1 lemon
2 tablespoons melted butter or margarine
1 teaspoon salt
$1/4$ teaspoon pepper
$1/4$ teaspoon marjoram
1 tablespoon minced parsley

(Firm and flavorful mackerel is justly popular)

Place mackerel, skin-side down, in greased broiler pan. Combine all other ingredients except parsley and spread half of mixture over fish. Broil until fish is tender and flakes easily, turn with spatula, spread remaining mixture over fish, and continue broiling until done.

TWELVE-MINUTE GRILL

Lemon-Broiled Mackerel. Recipe above.
Grilled Corn on Cob. Recipe 162, but eliminate garlic.
Cheese-Filled Mushrooms. Recipe 166. Broil corn and
    mushrooms alongside fish. Serve together.

146. BROILED SALMON STEAK WITH BROCCOLI

12-15 minutes in preheated broiler

About 3" from heat (2nd shelf in most broilers)

4 servings

4 salmon steaks (about 1½ pounds)
3 tablespoons melted butter or margarine
2 tablespoons lemon juice
1 teaspoon salt
2 cups cooked broccoli
1 cup medium white sauce

> *(Frozen steaks will need a few minutes longer under the broiler)*

Place steaks in broiler pan. Mix butter or margarine, lemon juice, and salt, and pour half the mixture over steaks. Broil on one side for about 6 minutes. Place the cooked broccoli alongside the fish in the pan and cover with white sauce. Turn steaks, pour rest of butter-lemon juice over them, and continue broiling until salmon is tender and white sauce is golden.

147. SALMON SCALLOP

6-10 minutes in preheated broiler

About 3" from heat (2nd shelf in most broilers)

Mix a can of flaked salmon with hot cooked noodles, and minced parsley or chives. Lay in greased shallow ovenware casserole and top with medium white sauce. Broil until sauce is hot and bubbly. Serve with potato chips for a quick supper.

148. SCROD OR POMPANO AMANDINE

7-10 minutes in preheated broiler

About 3" from heat (2nd shelf in most broilers)

4 servings

$1\frac{1}{2}$ pounds cod or pompano fillets
4 tablespoons melted butter
1 teaspoon salt
$\frac{1}{8}$ teaspoon pepper
$\frac{1}{2}$ cup slivered blanched almonds

(Scrod is cod that hasn't grown up)

Place fillets in greased broiler pan. Brush both sides with butter, and broil. Just before fish is done, season with salt and pepper; top with almonds. (You can buy canned slivered almonds.) Broil until barely brown. Turning is not necessary.

149. BROILED SHAD ROE

8-12 minutes in preheated broiler

3"-5" from heat (2nd or 3rd shelf in most broilers)

4 servings

4 small shad roe
1/4 cup melted butter or margarine
1 tablespoon lemon juice
1 teaspoon salt
Dash of pepper

(If you use larger roe, parboil first)

Wash and dry roe. Place in greased broiler pan. Combine other ingredients and brush some of the mixture over roe. Broil until brown, turning once. Brush roe several times with lemon mixture during the broiling. Serve with lemon wedges and garnish with parsley, if you like.

ALL-IN-ONE PLATE

Broiled Shad Roe. Recipe above.
Baked Idaho Broil. Recipe 175, but do not use cheese.
String Beans with Cheese. Recipe 185. Arrange potatoes and string beans on rack alongside roe, after it has been turned.

150. BROILED TROUT OR SMELTS MEUNIÈRE

8-10 minutes in preheated broiler

About 3" from heat (2nd shelf in most broilers)

4 servings

8 small dressed trout or smelts
2 tablespoons flour
1 teaspoon salt
1/4 teaspoon pepper
1/4 cup melted butter
1 tablespoon lemon juice
1 tablespoon minced parsley

(Melt butter in ovenware dish while preheating broiler)

Roll trout in flour seasoned with salt and pepper. Place in greased broiler pan. Pour half the butter over fish and broil until barely brown (about 4 minutes). Turn. Pour rest of butter and the lemon juice over fish and continue broiling until done. Sprinkle with parsley and serve.

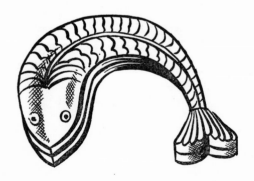

151. READY TO HEAT FROZEN FISH

5-10 minutes in preheated broiler

About 3" from heat (2nd shelf in most broilers)

Many kinds of frozen fried and breaded fish are on the market. Codfish cakes, smelts, oysters, flounder, perch, haddock, crab cakes, and deviled crab, even mixed fish grills, are available. Heat them under the broiler for a few minutes (see package directions) and serve with tartare or tomato sauce. For a quick dinner, broil frozen potato puffs and tomatoes with the fish.

152. STUFFED CRABS AU GRATIN

5-8 minutes in preheated broiler

About 3" from heat (2nd shelf in most broilers)

4 servings

1 pound cooked or canned crab meat
2 tablespoons melted butter
2 tablespoons flour
1 cup light cream
Salt and pepper
4 tablespoons grated **Parmesan cheese**

(Or broil in patty shells or ramekins)

Mix together crab meat, butter, flour, cream, salt and pepper. Fill crab shells with the mixture. Top each with 1 tablespoon of grated cheese. Broil on rack until brown.

153. BROILED STUFFED LOBSTER

15-20 minutes in preheated broiler

About 5" from heat (3rd shelf in most broilers)

Allow 1-1½ pounds for each serving

If possible, buy live lobster just before using, and have the dealer split it for you. If you *must* do it yourself, here are the steps:

1. Lay the lobster on its back on a wooden board. Cross the large claws; then hold them firmly with the left hand.

2. With a sharp pointed knife in the right hand, make a deep cut beginning at the mouth and drawing the knife quickly through the body and tail, to the back shell, until the lobster is opened.

3. Remove the dark intestinal vein, liver, stomach (small sac at back of head) and lungs (spongy mass at the sides). Discard everything but the green liver.

4. Crack large claws so that they open as flat as possible.

Now broil the lobster, cut-side down, on rack for about 8 minutes. Turn, and stuff cavity. Dot with butter, and continue broiling, adding butter if necessary, until lobster is golden brown. Serve with lots of melted butter.

4 tablespoons fine bread crumbs
½ teaspoon salt
Dash of pepper
Lobster liver
½ teaspoon lemon juice
2 tablespoons melted butter

Mix all ingredients and stuff lobster.

154. BOILED LOBSTER BROIL

8-12 minutes in preheated broiler

About 3" from heat (2nd shelf in most broilers)

Allow 1-1½ pounds for each serving

Cook the lobster by dropping it, head first, into boiling salted water to cover. Bring water back to boiling, cover, and boil for about 8 minutes. When cooked, remove from water, open each lobster and broil, flesh-side up, with or without stuffing as in Recipe 153. Do not turn. If you do not stuff, baste fish with lots of butter mixed with mashed garlic clove and minced parsley.

155. LOBSTER EN BROCHETTE

8-12 minutes in preheated broiler

About 5" from heat (3rd shelf in most broilers)

6 servings

1½ pounds raw or canned lobster meat
18 mushroom caps
¼ cup melted butter
1 tablespoon minced parsley
½ teaspoon lemon juice
Salt
Pepper

(Or use tomato wedges in place of mushroom caps)

Cut lobster meat into 2-inch squares. String on 8-inch skewers alternating with mushroom caps. Mix butter, parsley, lemon juice, salt, and pepper, and brush over skewers. Broil, turning as necessary, until lobster is lightly browned. Serve hot with more butter and tomato slices. French-fries, too.

156. JUMBO SHRIMP EN BROCHETTE

Have jumbo shrimps boiled, shelled and cleaned. On a skewer, string alternately shrimp and large pitted green olives. Repeat to fill skewer. Heat in broiler, and serve with tartare sauce or spicy cocktail sauce.

157. BROILED OYSTERS

5-8 minutes in preheated broiler

About 3" from heat (2nd shelf in most broilers)

4-6 oysters for each serving

Clean, drain, and dry oysters. Dip in slightly-beaten egg, then in seasoned buttered bread crumbs. Repeat dipping process. Broil, turning once, until oysters are golden on both sides. Dot with butter before broiling if you like.

In Blankets. Wrap each oyster in a bacon slice. Fasten with a pick, and broil until the bacon is crisp.

In Mushrooms. Select large mushrooms. Remove stems and dip mushrooms in melted butter, margarine, or oil. Broil, round-side up, for 2 minutes. Season with salt and pepper, and turn. Place an oyster in each mushroom hollow, cover with buttered bread crumbs, and broil for about 5 minutes more, or until oysters are golden.

WINTER PARTY LUNCHEON

Broiled Oysters in Mushrooms. Recipe above.

Asparagus in White Sauce. Recipe 185. Broil alongside oysters.

Chili Toast. Recipe 28. Toast alongside oysters and asparagus for the last few minutes of cooking, or on grill top if you have one.

158. OYSTERS CASINO

5-8 minutes in preheated broiler

About 3" from heat (2nd shelf in most broilers)

4 servings

24 oysters
Salt and pepper
2 tablespoons minced green pepper
2 tablespoons minced pimiento
4 slices bacon, minced
Lemon wedges

(A popular and quick recipe)

Open oysters and leave on deeper half of shell. Arrange shells on broiler rack (or in a shallow ovenware dish in a layer of coarse salt to hold shells steady). Sprinkle each oyster with salt, pepper, green pepper, and pimiento. Top with bacon. Broil until bacon is crisp and oyster edges begin to curl.

SEAFOOD GRILL

Oysters Casino. Recipe above.
Crab Cakes. Recipe 151.
Ready-to-Eat Fried Codfish Balls. Recipe 151.

> Buy small fried codfish balls and crab cakes at frozen food counter. Heat them in the broiler, and keep them warm in the grill if you have one (or in the bottom of the broilers). Broil oysters 5-8 minutes. Serve all together.

159. SCALLOPS IN HOT TARTARE SAUCE

10-15 minutes in preheated broiler

About 3" from heat (2nd shelf in most broilers)

4 servings

1 pound scallops
½ cup mayonnaise
1 tablespoon minced onion
1 tablespoon minced olive
1 tablespoon minced sweet pickle
1 tablespoon minced fresh parsley
1 tablespoon minced capers
2 tablespoons vinegar
1 teaspoon salt
¼ teaspoon pepper

> *(You may substitute sweet relish for the pickle and olive)*

Place scallops in greased broiler pan. Broil, turning once, until golden on both sides. Mix together all other ingredients and spread on scallops. Continue broiling until sauce is tinged brown.

vegetables can be wonderful

Pity the poor vegetable. Almost nobody loves it—that rejected little bit hiding its vitamins in a lot of water. Soon it will be a leftover, and less loved than ever.

Like other wallflowers, vegetables appreciate attention. A touch of white sauce on the spinach, a bright ribbon of pimiento, and cooked in the broiler, you have a dish to be proud of. Or asparagus, topped with bread crumbs, touched with butter; or canned peas, festive in a cream sauce made partly of the vegetable liquid. And how you can dress up cabbage! A suggestion of cayenne, a bit of butter, and you may talk of cabbages fit for kings.

So let your broiler work for you on leftover vegetables. Soon it would take my favorite story detective (Perry Mason of course), to recognize in those colorful family favorites the *Case of the Leftover Vegetable*.

160. BROILER-GLAZED CARROTS

8-10 minutes in preheated broiler

About 5" from heat (3rd shelf in most broilers)

4 servings

3 tablespoons honey
3 tablespoons grated American cheese
4 large cooked carrots

(An appealing dish, and filled with vitamins too)

Combine honey and cheese. Dip carrots into mixture and arrange in a shallow ovenware dish, or on aluminum foil, or in greased broiler pan. Broil until cheese melts.

HEARTY MAIN DISH

Broiler-Glazed Carrots. Recipe above.
Stuffed Peppers Caribbean. Recipe 170.
Duchesse Potatoes. Recipe 176.

     Broil 8 pepper halves for 4 minutes. Arrange carrots and potatoes in pan alongside peppers, and continue broiling until done.

161. CORN CAKES

8-10 minutes in preheated broiler

About 5" from heat (3rd shelf in most broilers)

12 patties

1½ cups sifted flour
2 teaspoons baking powder
½ teaspoon salt
2 eggs, well beaten
¼ cup milk
2 cups canned whole kernel corn

*(Real good with Canadian-style bacon broiled
at the same time)*

Sift together flour, baking powder, and salt. Combine eggs and milk, then pour into dry ingredients. Beat until smooth. Stir corn into this batter. Shape into patties, and broil until brown on heavily-greased broiler pan. Serve with maple sirup or honey.

162. GARLIC-GRILLED CORN ON COB

5-8 minutes in preheated broiler

About 3" from heat (2nd shelf in most broilers)

In a kettle, cook fresh or frozen corn on cob until tender. Then roll in lots of butter, season with garlic salt, and broil on rack until ears are lightly brown all over, turning as necessary.

163. EGGPLANT PATTIES

10-12 minutes in preheated broiler

About 5″ from heat (3rd shelf in most broilers)

8-10 patties

1 small eggplant, pared and cooked
½ teaspoon salt
Dash pepper
½ cup fine bread crumbs
Dash grated nutmeg

(Cook eggplant in boiling salted water to cover)

Chop fine cooked eggplant. Add the other ingredients, shape into patties, and broil on greased broiler rack until brown, turning once.

164. BREADED BROILED EGGPLANT SLICES

12-16 minutes in preheated broiler

About 5″ from heat (3rd shelf in most broilers)

Pare raw eggplant and cut into slices ½ inch thick. Dip in slightly-beaten egg, and then in bread crumbs. Broil in greased broiler pan until tender, turning once. If eggplant is not tender, set pan one shelf lower, and continue broiling. Season with salt and pepper, sprinkle with chopped chives, and serve hot.

165. GRILLED EGGPLANT WITH ANCHOVIES

10-16 minutes in preheated broiler

About 5" from heat (3rd shelf in most broilers)

Pare raw eggplant and cut into slices ½ inch thick. Marinate for 15 minutes in enough French dressing to cover. Season with salt and pepper, and cover slices with anchovy paste. Cook in broiler pan. Turn, and spread other side with anchovy paste. Continue broiling until tender. Serve with lemon wedges and, if you wish, with hot tomato sauce.

166. CHEESE-FILLED MUSHROOMS

5-7 minutes in preheated broiler

About 3" from heat (2nd shelf in most broilers)

Remove stems from large mushrooms, and peel if tough. Dip caps in melted butter, margarine, or other fat. Broil, hollow-side down for about 3 minutes. Then turn, dot with butter, and season with salt and pepper. Fill caps with crumbled Roquefort cheese mixed with equal amounts of minced celery. Top with fine bread crumbs. Sprinkle cayenne pepper over all. Broil until browned.

167. SHRIMP-FILLED MUSHROOMS

Follow Recipe 166 but fill mushroom caps with minced cooked shrimp moistened with white sauce. Garnish with minced chives and broil until lightly browned.

168. CHICKEN-FILLED MUSHROOMS AMANDINE

Follow Recipe 166 but fill mushroom caps with chopped cooked chicken, mixed with tiny cooked peas, moistened with cream, and topped with chopped almonds. Excellent for luncheon, served with toast points and broiled bacon.

169. BROILED ONION RINGS

6-10 minutes in preheated broiler

About 5" from heat (3rd shelf in most broilers)

Slice large Bermuda onions very thin. Dip in oil, sprinkle with salt and pepper, dip in cracker crumbs, and broil until browned.

170. STUFFED PEPPERS CARIBBEAN

12-15 minutes in preheated broiler

About 5" from heat (3rd shelf in most broilers)

4-8 servings

4 green peppers
1 small onion, minced
3 tablespoons oil
1 cup ground raw beef
½ teaspoon salt
Dash pepper
1 cup cooked rice
¾ cup tomato sauce
Chopped basil

*(Add grated American cheese for last few minutes
of broiling)*

Cut peppers in half lengthwise and discard seeds and membrane. Parboil for 3 minutes, then drain. Cook onion in oil until tender, add the beef, salt and pepper, and let brown. Add rice, tomato sauce, and basil. Fill peppers with mixture and arrange in broiler pan. Broil until peppers are brown. Add more tomato sauce during broiling if the peppers seem dry. Serve two halves for a luncheon dish, or one half as a side dish.

171. CRUNCHY SWEET POTATO-PINEAPPLE PUDDING

4-6 minutes in preheated broiler

About 5" from heat (3rd shelf in most broilers)

6 servings

6 hot sweet potatoes, mashed
1 cup drained crushed pineapple
3 tablespoons pineapple juice
3 tablespoons chopped nuts
6 quartered marshmallows

(A satisfying side dish for winter meals)

Combine all ingredients except marshmallows. Place in greased broiler pan or ovenware loaf pan, and broil until sweet potatoes are lightly browned. In the last minute, top with marshmallows and let them brown. Spoon out pudding and serve hot.

QUICK AND DELICIOUS GRILL

Broiled Ham Slices. Recipe 94. Place 6 cooked ham slices on broiler pan and place in preheated broiler. Cover with rack.

Crunchy Sweet-Potato-Pineapple Pudding. Recipe 171. Set pudding in ovenware pan on rack and heat as directed.

Orange Slices. Slice navel oranges crosswise, dust with brown sugar, arrange on pan alongside pudding, and broil at the same time. Do not turn.

172. HONEYED YAMS

12-15 minutes in preheated broiler

About 5" from heat (3rd shelf in most broilers)

4 servings

1 No. 2 can yams or sweet potatoes in sirup
2 tablespoons honey
1 teaspoon cinnamon
¼ teaspoon salt

(Or use 2½ cups freshly cooked instead of canned yams)

Drain yams or sweet potatoes and arrange in shallow oven-ware dish. Reserve ¼ cup sirup, mix with other ingredients, and pour over yams. Broil until sweet potatoes are lightly glazed and brown.

173. FROZEN FRENCH FRIED POTATOES

8-12 minutes in preheated broiler

About 3" from heat (2nd shelf in most broilers)

Arrange the bought potatoes in the broiler pan or on a sheet of aluminum foil. (Potatoes will fall through rack.) Broil until browned, turning once.

174. FROZEN POTATO PUFFS

8-12 minutes in preheated broiler

3"-5" from heat (2nd or 3rd shelf in most broilers)

Place the bought potato puffs in the pan or on the rack. Broil until evenly browned, turning once. Sprinkle with caraway seeds, salt to taste, and serve. Couldn't be easier!

175. BAKED IDAHO BROIL

3-5 minutes in preheated broiler

About 5" from heat (3rd shelf in most broilers)

Cut freshly-baked Idahos in half lengthwise, remove potato, and mash with butter, milk, salt, pepper, and minced parsley. Put back into skins, pile high in the center, and brown under broiler. Top with grated cheese before broiling, if you like. Serve hot.

176. POTATO CAKES

8-12 minutes in preheated broiler

About 3" from heat (2nd shelf in most broilers)

Season mashed potatoes with grated onion, salt, pepper, and parsley flakes, and shape into patties. Dip in fine bread crumbs and broil in pan until hot and brown, turning once.

177. DUCHESSE POTATOES

8-12 minutes in preheated broiler

3"-5" from heat (2nd or 3rd shelf in most broilers)

4-5 servings

4 cups mashed potatoes (about 6 medium)
4 tablespoons butter or margarine
1 teaspoon salt
2 eggs, well beaten
1 teaspoon chopped chives
Milk or cream to moisten
Butter

> *(For a festive look, squeeze potatoes through a pastry tube)*

Mix all ingredients until smooth. Then shape into mounds. Place in aluminum foil or greased ovenware cups, or directly in hot greased broiler pan, and top with butter. Broil until brown.

178. POTATO JAMBOREE

8-12 minutes in preheated broiler

About 3" from heat (2nd shelf in most broilers)

Cut cooked potatoes into slices about ¼ inch thick. Arrange in layers in shallow ovenware dish. Spread butter and grated cheese over each layer. Broil until cheese is bubbly and brown.

179. GARLIC-BROILED POTATO SLICES

15-20 minutes in preheated broiler

About 5" from heat (3rd shelf in most broilers)

Cut pared raw potatoes into slices about ¼-inch thick. Mash garlic, add melted butter, margarine, or oil, and brush on potato slices. Broil in pan or on rack until brown.

180. STUFFED SQUASH

10-15 minutes in preheated broiler

About 5" from heat (3rd shelf in most broilers)

4 servings

2 large summer squash
1½ cups creamed mushrooms
4 tablespoons chopped almonds
Salt and pepper

(A prepare-ahead dish for club days)

Cut squash in half lengthwise. Scoop out pulp leaving a quarter-inch shell. Cook pulp in just enough boiling water to cover bottom of saucepan. When tender, drain, combine with creamed mushrooms and almonds, season to taste with salt and pepper, and pile back into shells. Broil on rack until tops are lightly browned. If you wish, sprinkle with chopped basil leaves before serving.

181. BROILED TOMATOES
A DOZEN WAYS

6-8 minutes in preheated broiler

3"-5" from heat (2nd or 3rd shelf in most broilers)

Cut small firm tomatoes in half crosswise, or use large firm tomatoes sliced 1½ inches thick. Season with salt and pepper and top with a teaspoon or two of these suggested seasonings. Broil until tomatoes are tender and brown.

1 teaspoon chopped chives mixed with fine bread crumbs and melted butter

Paper-thin onion slice and ½ teaspoon prepared mustard

1 teaspoon grated cheese and a dash of cayenne pepper

1 teaspoon butter or oil with a clove of garlic, mashed and peeled, and ¼ teaspoon chopped parsley

1 teaspoon French dressing and a dash of tarragon

1 teaspoon Madeira wine and ½ teaspoon melted butter

1 teaspoon lemon juice, 1 teaspoon fine bread crumbs, and a squeeze of anchovy paste

1 teaspoon oil and ¼ teaspoon celery seed

1 teaspoon tarragon vinegar, 1 teaspoon chopped green pepper, dash of onion juice

1 teaspoon butter creamed with a dash of curry powder

1 teaspoon dry corn meal mixed with prepared mustard

Bread crumbs seasoned with powdered ginger and sugar

182. HOW TO PREPARE TOMATOES FOR STUFFING

Cut slice from stem end of tomato, scoop out pulp (save it for other uses) and drain tomato by turning it upside down for a few minutes. Season inside with salt, pepper, and dill or marjoram or basil or thyme or chervil or orégano. Then fill.

183. TOMATOES STUFFED WITH POTATOES

10-12 minutes in preheated broiler

About 5" from heat (3rd shelf in most broilers)

Prepare tomatoes for stuffing, Recipe 182, then fill with creamed cooked potatoes, top with breadcrumbs or grated cheese, and broil until tomatoes are tender.

184. VEGETABLE KEBAB

5-8 minutes in preheated broiler

About 3" from heat (2nd shelf in most broilers)

On skewers, string a tomato wedge, a square of green pepper, 1 pearl onion. Repeat until skewer is completely strung. Brush with butter, margarine, or oil, and season with celery salt. Broil until tomato is tender.

185. COOKED VEGETABLES 3 WAYS

4-8 minutes in preheated broiler

3"-5" from heat (2nd or 3rd shelf in most broilers)

Fresh-cooked or canned asparagus, broccoli, Brussels sprouts, cabbage, carrots, cauliflower, celery, corn, Lima beans, noodles, peas, pepper, potatoes, rice, spinach, squash, string beans, are some of the vegetables you can use in these recipes. Season them with salt and pepper first; arrange in shallow ovenware dishes; then follow these suggestions:

In tomato sauce. Use about ¾ cup of canned tomato sauce for 1 cup of cooked vegetables. Top vegetables with sauce, then sprinkle with crumbled cooked bacon. Heat in broiler.

In white sauce. Make a medium white sauce (about ¾ cup for 1 cup of cooked vegetables) using your own recipe, but substitute vitamin-rich vegetable liquid for some of the milk. Mix vegetables with sauce, cover with bread crumbs, and heat in broiler.

With cheese. Dot cooked vegetables with butter, sprinkle generously with grated cheese, and heat in broiler until cheese melts.

fruits for garnish and dessert

Grilled fruits will extend a scanty serving of meat or fish, add color to a plate, and give a planned air to an impromptu meal. They are undemanding too, for they may be broiled on any shelf, in a preheated or cold broiler, and are not likely to burn, even if neglected for a few minutes.

The gourmet's choice as a garnish for game has usually been grilled fruit. Broiled orange slices with duck, curried apple rings with goose, are standbys. But your imagination will suggest other possibilities. For instance, skewer chunks of candied ginger with pearl onions, heat in the broiler, and serve with a chicken grill. Chopped peanuts in a pear hollow, or chutney on a pineapple slice, broiled and served with a curry dish, will lend flavor and interest.

And there is a wide range of desserts too. Follow these recipes, or vary them, serve with cream, or hot sirup, or a sauce, or a meringue browned in the broiler, and you will have many perfect endings to your meals.

186. CURRIED APPLE SLICES

5-8 minutes in preheated broiler

About 3″ from heat (2nd shelf in most broilers)

Wash and core a tart apple (pare it too if you like). Cut into slices 1 inch thick. Make a paste by creaming together 1 tablespoon brown sugar, 1 tablespoon butter, and ½ teaspoon curry powder. Spread on one side of apple slice and broil until tender. Serve 1 or 2 slices as garnish.

187. APPLE SANDWICH

5-8 minutes in preheated broiler

About 3″ from heat (2nd shelf in most broilers)

Wash, pare, and core apples and cut into slices ¼ inch thick. Place a slice of American cheese between apple slices, and trim cheese to fit. Broil until apple is tender, turning once. Serve as garnish, sprinkled with ground nutmeg or cinnamon.

188. APPLE FRITTERS

5-8 minutes in preheated broiler

About 3" from heat (2nd shelf in most broilers)

4 servings

2 large eating apples
3 tablespoons brown sugar
2 tablespoons flour
¼ teaspoon baking powder
1 egg
Milk

(Use the batter for pineapple, banana, or other fruit fritters)

Wash, pare and core apples. Slice crosswise into rings ½ inch thick. Sprinkle with brown sugar. Make a batter of flour, baking powder, egg, and enough milk to produce the consistency of thick cream. Dip apple slices into batter, then broil on well-greased pan until brown on both sides, turning once. Drain on paper towel and serve sprinkled with powdered sugar.

SATISFYING ENDING

Apple Fritters With Coconut-Pecan Frosting. Recipe above. Just before fritters are done, top with frosting, recipe 194. Use only half of indicated amount.

189. APPLE MACAROON RINGS

4-7 minutes in preheated broiler

About 3" from heat (2nd shelf in most broilers)

4 servings

Wash, core, and pare if you like, 2 large eating apples. Slice crosswise into rings ½ inch thick. Place on broiler rack, dot with butter, sprinkle lightly with ground mace, and broil until golden. Turn, brush rings on other side with butter, sprinkle heavily with macaroon crumbs, and continue broiling until golden.

DESSERT SMÖRGASBORD

Apple Macaroon Rings. Recipe above.
Minted Pears. Recipe 200.
Party-Pretty Pineapple Slices. Recipe 201.

> Arrange fruit on pan. Broil all at the same time. Serve for dessert on one large platter; let guests help themselves.

190. ORANGE-FLAVORED APPLE BROIL

8-12 minutes in preheated broiler

About 5" from heat (3rd shelf in most broilers)

4 servings

4 baking apples
1 cup sugar
1 cup orange juice
4 teaspoons chopped nuts

*(Busy day hint: Cook apples and sirup ahead and
broil at the last minute)*

Wash apples, core and pare away an inch strip around the stem end. Boil sugar and juice in a large saucepan for a few minutes. *Stand* apples in this sirup, cover, and let them simmer gently for 12 to 15 minutes, or until tender.

Place apples on broiler pan, fill centers with nuts, and broil on rack until they are touched with gold. While apples are broiling, let sirup simmer in saucepan. If convenient, baste apples with sirup once or twice as they broil. When apples are done, pour thickened sirup over them. (Most broilers can hold 12 apples.)

191. BROILED CANNED APRICOTS

5-8 minutes in preheated broiler

About 3" from heat (2nd shelf in most broilers)

Brush drained, canned whole apricots with butter, sprinkle with brown sugar, and heat in broiler. Meanwhile, in a saucepan cook down apricot sirup to about half, and serve it hot over the broiled apricots.

192. FLUTED BROILED BANANAS

5-8 minutes in preheated broiler

About 3" from heat (2nd shelf in most broilers)

Allow 1 banana for each serving

Select firm, yellow or green-tinged bananas. Peel and flute by running the tines of a fork down the sides from top to bottom. Repeat until the whole banana is marked. Place in greased broiler pan. Brush with butter, sprinkle with sugar, and broil.

PRETTY DESSERT PLATE

Broiled Canned Apricots. Recipe 191.
Fluted Broiled Bananas. Recipe above.
Cream-Cheese Pineapple Slice. Recipe 201.

> Arrange fruit on pan. (Or if broiler is filled and you have a grill top, use it.) Broil all fruit at the same time. Serve on large platter.

193. FRUIT AMBROSIA

5-8 minutes in preheated broiler

3" from heat (2nd shelf in most broilers)

Peel all yellow or green-flecked bananas and cut in half lengthwise. Arrange them around the inside of a shallow ovenware serving dish. (A fluted glass pie plate to serve on a handsome wrought iron trivet might be used.) Overlap canned pineapple slices to fill the center of the dish. Place peeled orange sections in open spaces, and a maraschino cherry in the middle. Sprinkle with brown sugar and broil until golden. Just before removing from broiler, sprinkle with grated coconut and let brown. Serve in baking dish.

194. COCONUT PECAN FROSTING

3-6 minutes in preheated broiler

5"-7" from heat (3rd or 4th shelf in most broilers)

1/2 cup shredded coconut
1/4 cup brown sugar
1/4 cup chopped pecans
3 tablespoons melted butter, margarine, or shortening
2 tablespoons heavy cream

(Other nuts may be substituted)

Combine all ingredients, and blend well. Spread on 6 cup cakes or over an 8-inch-square cake. Broil until the frosting is bubbly and brown.

195. BROILED KADOTA FIGS

2-5 minutes in preheated broiler

3"-5" from heat (2nd or 3rd shelf in most broilers)

Fill drained canned Kadota figs with broken pecans or other nuts, roll in graham-cracker crumbs, and broil until crumbs are brown, turning once. Allow 3 or 4 for each serving, as dessert.

196. RICE-STUFFED FIGS

3-5 minutes in preheated broiler

3"-5" from heat (2nd or 3rd shelf in most broilers)

Fill drained canned figs with cooked rice, sprinkle with powdered cloves, and heat in the broiler. Allow 2 or 3 for each serving of chicken, meat, or fish.

197. BROILED GRAPEFRUIT 4 WAYS

10-15 minutes in cold broiler

3"-5" from heat (2nd or 3rd shelf in most broilers)

Cut grapefruit in half. Loosen sections by cutting inside each with a sharp knife. Pour any of the following over each half, place on broiler rack or pan, and broil until edges of grapefruit are lightly browned.

KIRSCH-FLAVORED. *Pour 2 tablespoons Kirsch over each half.*

NUTMEG-SEASONED. *Sprinkle each half with nutmeg and add a tablespoon of honey.*

PINEAPPLE-FILLED. *Add 1 tablespoon crushed pineapple to each half.*

VERMONT STYLE. *Dot grapefruit half with butter and pour maple sirup over it.*

BREAKFAST COOKED AT THE TABLE

Vermont Style Grapefruit. Recipe above. Broil on aluminum foil. Broil this first. Serve.

Lots of French Toast. Recipe 29. Remove foil and broil toast on pan.

Pineapple Pigs on a Skewer. Wrap pineapple wedges in bacon strips, secure with picks. Broil alongside French toast. Serve together.

198. ORANGE CUPS

8-10 minutes in preheated broiler

3"-5" from heat (2nd or 3rd shelf in most broilers)

6 servings

6 large orange halves
3 cups canned apricot halves drained
1 tablespoon grated orange peel
3 tablespoons apricot sirup
¼ teaspoon grated nutmeg
2 tablespoons honey

*(Cooked peaches instead of apricots will make a
luscious cup too)*

Remove pulp from oranges (save for other uses). Combine
all other ingredients, except honey, and fill orange shells.
Cover tops with honey and heat in broiler.

BRUNCH IN THE PATIO

Orange Cups. Recipe above. Serve as first course.
Chicken Livers on Toast. Now broil chicken livers (allow 2 for each serving). Serve on buttered toast
made on grill-top, or alongside the livers in the
broiler. Livers will be ready in 6-10 minutes.
Hot Coffee. Make it ahead. Keep it hot on the grill.

199. BROILED PEACHES 4 WAYS

5-10 minutes in preheated broiler

3"-5" from heat (2nd or 3rd shelf in most broilers)

Use large ripe fresh peaches (pared, halved, pitted) or canned peach halves, drained. Lay on broiler rack or pan, cut-side up, fill with any of the following, and broil until edges of peaches are lightly browned.

CHERRY-FILLED. *Sprinkle peaches with cinnamon, and fill hollows with canned Bing cherries.*

CRUNCHY. *Fill peach hollows with chopped nuts, top with shredded coconut, and broil until coconut is lightly browned. Watch this, coconut browns quickly!*

TARTARE. *Put a tablespoon of mayonnaise in each peach hollow.*

TWO-FLAVORED. *Fill each hollow with equal parts of apricot jam and honey.*

200. BROILED PEARS 4 WAYS

5-8 minutes in preheated broiler

About 3" from heat (2nd shelf in most broilers)

Drain large canned pears or cut ripe ones in half and remove cores. Fill hollows with any of the following and broil on rack or pan until edges of pears are slightly browned.

SHERRY. *Add a tablespoon of sherry wine to each hollow.*

MINTED. *Fill each hollow with mint jelly and sprinkle with sugar.*

PEPPER-FILLED. *Add 1 tablespoon minced green pepper to each hollow and sprinkle with nutmeg.*

ROQUEFORT. *Fill hollow with crumbled Roquefort or blue cheese and broil until cheese is browned.*

201. BROILED PINEAPPLE SLICES 4 WAYS

5-10 minutes in preheated broiler

3"-5" from heat (2nd or 3rd shelf in most broilers)

Place canned drained pineapple slices on broiler rack or pan, spread with any of the following, and broil until edges of pineapple begin to brown.

BANANA SPREAD. *Mash bananas with butter and spread on pineapple slices.*

CREAM CHEESE. *Mix cream cheese with enough pineapple sirup to make smooth paste. Spread on pineapple slices and dust with cinnamon.*

HONEY-TOPPED. *Dot pineapple slices with butter and sprinkle with honey.*

PARTY-PRETTY. *Insert a maraschino cherry in each pineapple slice and spread with shredded coconut. (Watch coconut, it browns quickly.)*

202. PINEAPPLE FRITTERS

5-8 minutes in preheated broiler

About 3" from heat (2nd shelf in most broilers)

Drain slices of canned pineapple. Follow Recipe 188 for the batter, dip pineapple into batter, then arrange on well-greased pan. Broil until golden, turning once. Serve sprinkled with powdered cloves if you wish.

203. SKEWERED FRUIT MEDLEY

4-10 minutes in preheated broiler

3"-5" from heat (2nd or 3rd shelf in most broilers)

On skewers about 6 inches long, string any of the following combinations, then dip in honey, or brown sugar, or melted butter, and heat in broiler.

1. Pineapple wedges, cooked but still firm pitted prunes, and thick orange sections, with a red maraschino cherry separating the fruits.

2. Cooked but still firm prunes, stuffed with cream cheese and chopped almonds, wrapped in half slice of bacon, alternated with pear chunks. Broil until bacon is crisp.

3. Cooked or canned but still firm apricots stuffed with Roquefort cheese, alternated with watermelon and pineapple wedges.

4. Apple wedges and pineapple slices separated by large seedless grapes. Broil until apple is soft.

5. Orange sections with, yes, little pearl onions. Heat in broiler for an excellent meat accompaniment.

Serve 2 skewers for each person at breakfast or dessert. Serve 1 skewer as meat or fish accompaniment. Stick them in a grapefruit, lay them on a plate with the points meeting in the center and fanning out at the rim, or find your own imaginative way to bring the skewers to the table.

the

rotisserie

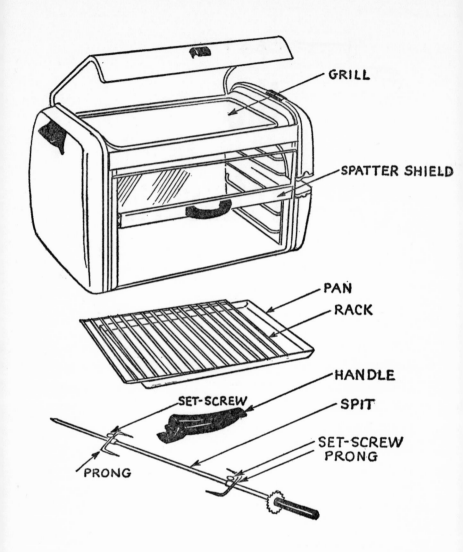

GRILL

SPATTER SHIELD

PAN

RACK

HANDLE

SET-SCREW

SPIT

SET-SCREW
PRONG

PRONG

about the rotisserie

The rotisserie is an electric appliance for roasting on a rotating spit. This defines the subject. The object is marvelous cooking, perhaps the best you have ever had. Until you have tried a spit-roast or a barbecued chicken, you might have doubts. Tasting resolves them all. The modern small rotisserie has all the advantages of the broiler—it is portable, smokeless, worksaving—and it has some extra attractions, too.

THE ADVANTAGES OF THE ROTISSERIE

Roasts are juicier. Since the roast is exposed directly to radiant heat, not baked by dry heat as in an oven, proteins coagulate at the surface, forming an outer wall which prevents much juice from escaping. Any that does is caught on the roast as it revolves, hence the advertised "sealed in flavor."

Fun when you entertain. Have you ever watched a crowd gather in front of a store window to watch a chef flipping pancakes? Your guests will find it just as fascinating to watch a roast revolve, see it brown, hear its sizzle, smell its goodness. By all means, show off your skill with a rotisserie next time you entertain.

Carving is easier. Since most roasts must be boned and rolled at the market before they are spitted, carving at the table is a quick and easy business. No spills, no delayed starts, no cold food.

You can cook 1 large roast or 2 chickens. Roasts weighing as much as 10 pounds, if the proper shape, can be spit-roasted. Or 2 small broiler-fryers can be barbecued at the same time.

HOW TO CARE FOR THE ROTISSERIE

The rotisserie is part of your broiler. Follow the 5 rules on page 13 for broiler care.

HOW TO USE THE ROTISSERIE

1. The first time you use the rotisserie, remove the spit, and mark it for easy centering of food, page 176.

2. Place pan, without rack, in the bottom of the rotisserie.

Take handle off, or rest it outside. To save washing, line the pan first with aluminum foil.

3. Turn on switch and preheat according to manufacturer's directions. Preheating is suggested to improve accuracy of timing. Generally, 4 to 10 minutes is the recommended preheating time.

4. Slip one adjustable locking prong on spit, prongs pointing in.

5. With the spit, spear food lengthwise *through the center*.

6. Center the roast under heating unit, page 176.

7. Slip second locking prong on spit, prongs pointing in. Push both prongs into the food, then tighten screws.

8. Insert spit into grooves following manufacturer's directions, hook on spatter shield to retain heat, and turn on switch to start the motor which operates the spit.

9. Check time charts or follow timing for individual recipe; set the automatic timer if you have one; then relax until the roast is done. Basting is not necessary. If you wish, by all means do it.

10. When meat is cooked, switch off motor, turn heat off, detach spatter shield, remove spit from grooves, loosen screws, and slide roast off spit, onto platter heated on rotisserie in last few minutes.

11. Use any drippings to make gravy, if you wish.

12. Soak spit, prongs, and slightly cooled pan in warm, soapy water. Rinse and dry.

HOW TO MARK SPIT FOR CENTERING FOOD

In most rotisseries, center of spit and center of heating coils do not coincide, because the spit is longer than the rotisserie. Since food must be centered under the heating coils to assure even roasting and turning, it is wise to mark the spit permanently and avoid laborious trials each time you roast. To make the center:

1. Place the spit in position in the rotisserie.

2. Tie strings around the spit where it meets the shelf supports on the left and right walls of the rotisserie.

3. Remove the spit, and with a small file, a nail, or a kitchen knife, make deep incisions in the spit where the strings are tied. The distance between incisions is the area of maximum heat. You can easily center food between your permanent markings. Be sure that prongs and screws are locked inside the incisions, otherwise they will catch on shelf-supports or walls as the spit revolves.

WHAT HEAT TO USE

If your rotisserie has 1 heat (approximately 1500 watts) use it for preheating and roasting, but reduce time given in the recipes and charts by 5 to 10 minutes for each pound of meat.

If your rotisserie has 2 heats (approximately 1500 watts or high; approximately 300 watts or low) use high heat for preheating and roasting, but reduce time given in the recipes and charts by 5 to 10 minutes for each pound of meat.

If your rotisserie has 3 heats (approximately 1500 watts or high; approximately 1000 watts or medium; approximately 300 watts or low) use medium heat for preheating and roasting. The time given in the recipes and charts is for medium heat, which is recommended for roasting as it results in the least shrinkage.

A word about low heat. If dinner must be delayed, turn heat to low, to slow up cooking and keep roast warm. Also, if you have time, start the roast at medium heat, then after half an hour or less, turn to low heat and so double (at least) the cooking time. This is not generally practical in our busy days, but a superbly tender and juicy roast, with almost no shrinkage, is the happy result.

USEFUL ACCESSORIES FOR SPIT-ROASTING

Lining the pan with *aluminum foil* saves washing. Buy a *long-handled pastry brush* or a *bulb-and-ovenware-glass baster* for basting. An *asbestos glove* for reaching into the rotisserie, *poultry skewers and laces*, and *poultry shears* are also great conveniences.

Some rotisseries are equipped with extra spits. One has a 4-spit accessory that is excellent for roasting small things, chicken livers, cocktail frankfurters, shrimps, oysters, and kebabs.

Another has a hinged revolving grill on a spit for cooking steaks, chops, frankfurters, and fish without hand-turning.

these roasts are superb

Gourmets say the best way to cook meat is by spit-roasting, which is entirely satisfactory to homemakers because it is easy too. Any roast tender enough for the oven and small enough to fit on the spit without touching the rotisserie walls or heating coils can be used. Most appliances can hold a roast 5 to 6 inches across, and perhaps 12 inches long, after boning and rolling. Roasts having large bones should be boned first.

It is not always necessary to baste since the flavor cannot penetrate very far into the meat. Only when a surface flavor or a glaze is desirable is basting suggested. But if you plan to serve gravies or sauces, do use any pan drippings in their preparation. Or why not warm cooked small potatoes, rice, or onion slices in the pan where they can catch the drippings?

204. ROLLED RIB ROAST

15-20 minutes per pound

Medium heat in preheated rotisserie

Allow ¼-⅓ pound for each serving

Order a first-grade cut, usually any of the ribs between short-loin and chuck. Have butcher bone, roll, tie beef. Roast should fit on the spit without touching heating coils or rotisserie walls, no more than 5 to 6 inches across, and about 12 inches long.

You may, if you wish, rub salt and pepper into the roast. However, since seasoning will not penetrate very far, and because it seems to me to draw out juices, I prefer to season after cooking. You may like to insert slivers of garlic into the roast to add flavor. Remove the garlic before serving.

Put spit lengthwise through center of roast and lock with prongs. Slip the spit into the rotisserie and roast until brown. Approximate cooking time:

Weight	*Total broiling time in hours*		
	RARE	MEDIUM	WELL DONE
3-4 pounds	1-1¼	1¼-1½	1½-1¾
5-6 pounds	1¼-1½	1½-1¾	1¾-2
7-8 pounds	1½-1¾	1¾-2	2 or more

205. ROLLED SIRLOIN OF BEEF

15-20 minutes per pound

Medium heat in preheated rotisserie

Allow ¼-⅓ pound for each serving

Buy this boned, rolled, and tied. If you wish, make small cuts in the roast and insert slivers of garlic. Remove the garlic before serving. Put spit lengthwise through center of roast and lock with prongs. Slip the spit into the rotisserie and roast until brown.

Use eye round or chuck roast also, and follow the time given in Recipe 204. If less tender cuts are roasted, let meat stand in the refrigerator for several hours in a tenderizing marinade, made by combining 2 parts oil and 1 part vinegar. Add herbs and mashed clove of garlic, if you wish, and baste the meat with the marinade every 15 minutes while it roasts.

Lean roasts should be wrapped in fat and tied before roasting. Pour fat out of the drip pan as it accumulates, or use a bulb-and-ovenware-glass baster to separate fat from juices. Serve the juice with the roast, of course.

For quicker roasting, use high heat.

206. VEAL AND PEPPERS

12-16 minutes

Medium heat in preheated rotisserie

3-4 servings

1½ pounds veal steak, cut ½-inch thick
1 teaspoon salt
¼ teaspoon pepper
2 large green peppers cut into 2-inch squares
¼ cup French dressing

(Try adding a mashed garlic clove to the dressing)

Cut veal into 2-inch squares, sprinkle with salt and pepper, and string on spit, alternating with pepper squares. Center under heating unit, lock with prongs, and brush with French dressing. Slip the spit into rotisserie with drip pan at the bottom. Broil until veal is brown, tender, and juicy. Serve on hot noodles, if you like.

FIRESIDE ROAST

Veal and Peppers. Recipe above.
Cherry-Filled Peaches. Recipe 199. Arrange peaches on pan, place pan just below veal, and broil while veal roasts. Serve together.

207. ROLLED SHOULDER OF VEAL

1½-2 hours

Medium heat in preheated rotisserie

7-8 servings

3 pounds boned veal shoulder
Lemon
Salt and pepper
Melted butter

(Serve with lemon butter mixed with chopped parsley)

Have veal boned at the market. Cut lemon and rub over surface of meat, season with salt and pepper, sprinkle with butter. Roll up and tie with string. Put veal on spit lengthwise, center, lock, rub lemon over outside, and brush with more butter. Roast until brown. Baste every 15 minutes with butter. Use a long-handled pastry brush. Do not turn off heat or motor when basting. Remove string and serve veal with cooked rice, seasoned, perhaps, with pan drippings.

SUPPER FOR THE GANG

Rolled Shoulder of Veal. Recipe above.
Noodles with Cheese. Recipe 185. Arrange noodles in
  shallow ovenware pan or in broiler pan. Broil for
  15 minutes as veal finishes roasting.

208. SPITTED LIVER

10-15 minutes

Medium heat in preheated rotisserie

4-6 servings

2 pounds beef or calf liver, cut 1-inch thick
12 slices bacon
3 sliced onions

(Serve with parsley-flavored toasted French bread)

Cut liver into 2-inch squares, wrap in bacon, then string pieces on spit, alternating with slices of onions. Center food under heating unit, lock with prongs, and roast until liver is brown, bacon is done, and onions are crisp. Heat bread on top of rotisserie.

LOW-CALORY GRILL

Spitted Liver. Recipe above.
Baked Idaho Broil. Recipe 175. Mash potatoes with skim milk, no butter.
Broiled Tomatoes. Recipe 181. Top tomatoes with grated onion, vinegar, chopped green pepper. Broil potatoes and tomatoes in pan while liver is on spit.

209. ROAST ROLLED LEG OF LAMB

1-1½-2 hours

Medium heat in preheated rotisserie

10-12 servings

6-pound leg of lamb, boned and rolled
1 clove garlic, peeled and mashed
2 teaspoons salt
½ teaspoon pepper
1 teaspoon sweet marjoram
1 teaspoon thyme
1 tablespoon oil

(Heat the serving platter on top of the rotisserie)

Have lamb boned and rolled at the market. Combine all other ingredients to make a paste. Rub the paste over the meat and let it stand for about an hour, then put lamb on spit, center it under heating unit, and be sure the drip pan is in place. Lock lamb with prongs, slip the spit into rotisserie; and roast until well done. When roast is done, slip it out of the rotisserie onto hot platter, unlock prongs, remove spit, and bring to table ready for carving.

210. MINTED LEG OF LAMB

Follow Recipe 209 but, using a long handled pastry brush, baste the lamb every 15 minutes while it roasts with a sauce made by cooking for 5 minutes: 1 cup sugar, 2 cups water, and ½ cup chopped mint leaves. Do not turn off heat or rotisserie motor while basting.

211. STUFFED LAMB SHOULDER

1¼-1½ hours

Medium heat in preheated rotisserie

6-8 servings

4-pound shoulder of lamb, boned
3 cups soft bread crumbs
½ teaspoon salt
⅛ teaspoon pepper
¼ teaspoon marjoram
2 tablespoons chopped parsley
½ teaspoon grated onion
⅓ cup melted butter

(You'll like this delicious stuffed lamb roast)

Have the lamb boned at the market. Combine all other ingredients. Spread this mixture on lamb, then roll it and tie with string. Put lamb on spit, center under heating unit, lock with prongs; slip the spit into rotisserie, and roast until meat is brown and tender. Then remove from rotisserie, unlock prongs, slip roast from spit, and serve on heated platter.

MIXED GRILL FOR SIX

Stuffed Lamb Shoulder. Recipe above.
Vegetable Kebab. Recipe 184. Allow one or two kebabs for each serving. Heat in broiler pan for 30 minutes as lamb finishes roasting.

212. SHISH KEBAB IN HERB MARINADE

Shaashlick or shish kebab, whatever you call it, these roasted chunks of meat are dramatic and exotic. Fun to say, to see, to taste.

15-25 minutes

Medium heat in preheated rotisserie

4 servings

1½ pounds lamb, cut ½-inch thick
¼ cup oil
2 tablespoons lemon juice
1 tablespoon grated onion
1 tablespoon chopped parsley
1 teaspoon sweet marjoram
1 teaspoon thyme
1 teaspoon salt
¼ teaspoon pepper
2 sliced firm tomatoes
2 sliced onions

(If you wish, baste the lamb with the marinade)

Cut lamb into 2½-inch squares. Let stand in refrigerator for several hours in a sauce made by combining oil, lemon juice, onion, parsley, marjoram, thyme, salt, and pepper. When ready to use, drain, and string on spit in the following order: lamb, tomato, lamb, onion; repeat for length of spit. Lock with prongs, slip the spit into the rotisserie, and roast until lamb is tender and brown; onion crisp. Serve on freshly cooked rice placed in broiler pan in last 5 minutes to catch lamb drippings.

213. SHISH KEBARBECUE

15-25 minutes

Medium heat in preheated rotisserie

4 servings

1½ pounds lamb, cut ½-inch thick
½ cup olive oil
2 tablespoons lemon juice
2 tablespoons chili sauce
2 tablespoons soy sauce
1 tablespoon ground coriander
1 teaspoon salt
1 clove garlic, peeled and mashed
4 tablespoons sherry
4 green peppers cut into 2½-inch squares

(Coriander makes this sauce different)

Cut lamb into 2½-inch squares. Let stand in refrigerator for several hours in a sauce made by combining all ingredients, except green pepper. When ready to cook, drain, and string lamb on spit, alternating it with green-pepper squares. Repeat for length of spit. Lock with prongs, slip the spit into rotisserie, and roast until lamb is brown, peppers crunchy.

214. ROAST PICNIC SHOULDER

1 ¾-2 ¼ hours

Medium heat in preheated rotisserie

10-12 servings

4-pound boned-and-rolled picnic pork shoulder
1 clove garlic
1 cup pineapple sirup
2 tablespoons brown sugar
Dash powdered cloves

(No pink should appear in the meat when done)

Buy the pork shoulder boned and rolled. Rub cut garlic over it. Put the shoulder on the spit, center it under the heating unit, and lock with prongs. Slip the spit into the rotisserie, and roast until done. In the last few minutes, warm serving platter on the rotisserie. When roast is done, slip it onto platter, unlock prongs, remove spit, and serve. In a saucepan, make a sauce by combining sirup, sugar and cloves; heat for a few minutes, and serve with roast.

HOLIDAY BUFFET FOR EIGHT

Roast Picnic Shoulder. Recipe above. Save leftovers for
   tomorrow.
Honeyed Yams. Double Recipe 172.
Apple Broil. Double Recipe 190.
   Broil yams and apples in broiler pan during last
   half hour of roasting time.

215. BONELESS SMOKED SHOULDER BUTT

35-45 minutes

Medium heat in preheated rotisserie

3-4 servings

2-pound ready-to-eat shoulder butt
Whole cloves
Prepared mustard

(Or use currant jelly instead of mustard)

Remove cellophane or stockinette wrapper from butt. Score it lightly into squares or diamonds. Stud with cloves. Put spit lengthwise through center of butt, and lock with prongs. Spread mustard over butt, slip the spit into the rotisserie, and roast until brown. Apple slices, sprinkled with brown sugar, may be cooked in pan during roasting.

TERRACE GRILL

Boneless Smoked Shoulder Butt. Recipe above.
Fluted Bananas. Recipe 192.
Green Pepper Rings. Use parboiled peppers. Brush with oil. Broil bananas and peppers in pan while butt roasts.

216. BARBECUED SPARERIBS

1 ¼-1 ¾ hours

Medium heat in preheated rotisserie

8-10 servings

5 pounds spareribs
1 cup catsup
1½ cups vinegar
4 tablespoons Worcestershire sauce
2 tablespoons prepared mustard
2 tablespoons brown sugar
2 teaspoons salt

(A piquant flavor makes this a favorite)

String spareribs on spit accordion style, lock with prongs, slip the spit into rotisserie, and roast for 15 minutes. Meanwhile, combine other ingredients in a saucepan and let cook for 15 minutes at low heat. Baste spareribs every 15 minutes with this sauce, until done.

217. CANADIAN-STYLE BACON

25-35 minutes

Medium heat in preheated rotisserie

4-6 servings

1-1½-pound piece Canadian-style bacon
¼ cup orange marmalade

*(For a quick dinner, heat cooked string beans and
tomato slices in pan)*

Remove wrapping from bacon. Put spit lengthwise through center of meat, and lock. Spread marmalade over bacon, slip spit into rotisserie, and roast until brown. Pineapple slices may be heated in pan during the roasting.

barbecued chicken and other birds

Barbecuing suggests two methods of cooking. It can mean roasting a whole bird by radiant heat, or cooking parts in a highly seasoned sauce. In this chapter, it is the whole bird we use.

Chicken on a spit is a handsome sight. Brushed with oil, it turns beautifully brown outside, while the inside remains tender and moist. If you have never tasted barbecued chicken, you have a treat in store. These recipes may be modified. You may have your own way with stuffings, dressings, or under-the-skin herb spreads. Do use them. The rotisserie will make your favorite dishes taste even better.

Before you barbecue, please read the sections on select-
ing, preparing, and trussing fowl. They are important.

HOW TO SELECT POULTRY FOR SPIT-ROASTING

Any bird which is tender enough for oven-roasting may be
spit-roasted, provided that it is small enough to fit your
rotisserie.

Chicken: Fresh, frozen (defrosted), or canned whole
young chicken may be used. Broiler-fryers
should weigh no more than 3½ pounds, and
roasters no more than 5½ pounds. Two broilers
weighing about 2 pounds each may be spit-
roasted at one time. Allow ¾ to 1 pound dressed
or ½ to ¾ pound ready-to-cook weight for
each serving.

Turkey: Junior turkeys weighing about 5 to 6 pounds
may be roasted. Allow ¾ to 1 pound dressed, or
½ to ¾ pound ready-to-cook weight for each
serving.

Duck: Young ducks for roasting should weigh no
more than 5 to 6 pounds. Allow 1 to 1¼ pounds
dressed, or ¾ to 1 pound ready-to-cook weight
for each serving.

Goose: A young goose may also be roasted. It should
weigh no more than 6 to 7 pounds. Allow about
2 pounds dressed, or 1¼ to 1½ pounds ready-
to-cook weight for each serving.

HOW TO PREPARE POULTRY FOR
SPIT-ROASTING

Most of the preparation is done at the market. After the bird is dressed (feathers removed, but head and feet still on), have it drawn for roasting (head, feet, and insides removed through an incision made in the body). Have the neck skin pulled back, and the neck cut off. (Save the giblets and the neck for other recipes.) Have the oil sac at the tail removed. When you get the bird home, wash it inside and out. Go over the insides to make certain cleaning has been thorough, and remove any pinfeathers. Dry and refrigerate, or use immediately.

HOW TO TRUSS POULTRY

After the bird is washed, dried, and stuffed (if it is going to be), it must be trussed to retain its shape, and assure even rotation and browning during the roasting. Here are the steps:

1. If the bird has been stuffed, close the body openings with poultry pins and cord, or sew them up with needle and thread.

2. Fold the wings, then tie them close to the body with heavy cord.

3. Tie the ends of the legs together with cord, then loop the cord around the tail and tie.

4. Insert the spit through the body cavity. Close any open-

ings made by the spit. (Skewer them, sew them, or tighten the cord.)

5. Center the bird under the heating unit, page 176, and lock it into place with the prongs. Catch ends of legs under prongs on one side.

6. Two small birds may be trussed in the same way. They should be placed on the spit with necks meeting and over-lapping under the center of the heating unit.

7. Brush generously with melted butter, margarine, oil, or other fat, and roast.

218. HOW TO ROAST CHICKEN
TO PERFECTION

1-1¼ hours

Medium heat in preheated rotisserie

4-6 servings

1 roasting chicken (4 pounds ready to cook)
   or 2 broiling chickens (each about 1½ pounds ready to cook)
Salt
Lots of melted butter, margarine, or oil

(Reduce broiling time if two chickens are used)

Quickly wash and dry chicken. Season inside with salt and brush with fat. If the bird is stuffed, close the body openings, truss, put on the spit, and lock. Now brush outsides with butter (a pastry brush makes the job easier). Slip the spit into rotisserie, and roast until chicken is evenly brown and done as you like it. Brush the chicken with fat every 20 minutes or so. Do not turn off heat or motor when basting. This is crisp, crackly, perfectly done chicken! Remove spit from rotisserie, and carve the bird while it is still on the spit. (Poultry shears are a good investment.)

NOTE ABOUT ROASTING CHICKEN

If chicken is about ready, but you are not, reduce heat to slow speed, and no one will be the wiser. May even improve the bird.

219. CHICKEN BURGUNDY

1-1¼ hours

Medium heat in preheated rotisserie

6 servings

1 whole roasting chicken (4 pounds ready to cook)
½ cup butter, margarine, or oil
½ cup Burgundy wine
1 teaspoon marjoram
1 teaspoon parsley
1 teaspoon salt
¼ teaspoon pepper

(Eggplant slices are delicious cooked in drip pan)

Wash chicken inside and out. Make a marinade of all the other ingredients, and let chicken stand in this, refrigerated, for several hours. Drain chicken (save the marinade). Truss, put on spit, and lock into position with prongs. Slip spit into rotisserie, with drip pan in place, and roast. Baste with marinade every 15 minutes until done, when drumstick, held with a paper towel, should be tender and move easily.

SUNDAY CHICKEN DINNER

Chicken Burgundy. Recipe above.
Stuffed Squash. Recipe 180. Increase if necessary.
Skewered Fruit Medley. Recipe 203, item 3. Arrange squash and skewers in broiler pan, and broil for 30 minutes as chicken finishes roasting. Serve together.

220. CHICKEN PAPRIKA

40-50 minutes

Medium heat in preheated rotisserie

4 servings

1   whole chicken (2½ pounds ready to cook)
1   lemon
1   clove garlic
1   teaspoon salt
¼   teaspoon pepper
2   tablespoons melted butter, margarine, or oil
1   tablespoon paprika

(Cook thin onion slices on drip pan during roasting)

Rub chicken inside and out with cut lemon and cut garlic. Sprinkle with salt and pepper. Mix butter or other fat with paprika and brush half of the mixture inside chicken. Truss, put bird on spit, and lock with prongs. Slip spit into rotisserie, put drip pan in place, and roast until chicken is tender, brushing several times with fat-paprika mixture.

DINNER COOKED AT THE TABLE

Chicken Paprika. Recipe above.
Garlic Corn on Cob. Recipe 162.
Pepper-Filled Pears. Recipe 200.
    Broil corn and pears in broiler pan for 30 minutes as chicken finishes roasting. Serve together.

221. CHINESE PINEAPPLE CHICKEN

40-50 minutes

Medium heat in preheated rotisserie

4 servings

1 whole chicken (2½ pounds ready to cook)
1 lemon
1 clove garlic
1 teaspoon salt
¼ teaspoon pepper
1 cup drained crushed pineapple
2 tablespoons cornstarch
1 tablespoon soy sauce
½ teaspoon powdered ginger (optional)
2 tablespoons melted butter, margarine, or oil
2 cups rice

(Pineapple adds a delightful flavor to this bird)

Rub chicken inside and out with cut lemon and cut garlic. Sprinkle with salt and pepper. Mix pineapple, cornstarch, soy sauce, and ginger, if you are using it. Spoon into cavity of the bird. Close the body openings, truss bird, put on spit, and lock with prongs. Center bird between marks on spit (page 176). Slip spit into the rotisserie, brush chicken with butter, margarine, or oil, and roast until done. Test drumstick (held in a paper towel) to be sure it is tender.

After you have put the chicken on a spit, cook the rice in a saucepan. About 10 to 15 minutes before the chicken is done, turn the rice into the pan to catch the chicken drippings. Add 2 or 3 tablespoons pineapple sirup, or more, if the rice appears to be drying. The rice will keep warm and have an intriguing flavor. Garnish with chopped chives.

222. ROAST DUCKLING WITH ORANGE STUFFING

1¼-1¾ hours

Medium heat in preheated rotisserie

4 servings

1 duckling (four pounds ready to cook)
¼ cup minced onion
2 cups minced celery
¼ cup butter, margarine, or oil
1 teaspoon salt
¼ teaspoon pepper
2½ cups fine bread crumbs
1 cup sliced oranges
1 tablespoon grated orange peel
½ cup orange juice

(If you like, baste every 15 minutes with orange juice)

Clean, wash, and dry bird. In a large saucepan, cook onion and celery in butter or other fat until soft. Add other ingredients, mix well, and turn into cavity of duck. Close the openings, truss wings, put bird on spit, and lock with prongs. Slip the spit into the rotisserie, with drip pan in place, and roast until tender and brown. Drumstick should be tender and move easily.

223. BARBECUED TURKEY WITH WALNUT STUFFING

2½-3 hours

Medium heat in preheated rotisserie

8 servings

1 whole junior turkey (5 pounds ready to cook)
1 teaspoon salt
¼ pound butter, melted on top of rotisserie

(Don't pack turkey too full—dressing expands)

Wipe bird inside and out. Rub with salt and fill with Walnut Stuffing. Close the openings, truss, put the turkey on the spit, and lock with prongs. Roast bird, basting every 15 minutes with butter. The turkey is done when drumstick feels tender (take hold with paper towel) and leg moves easily.

WALNUT STUFFING

½ cup butter, margarine, or other fat
1 large onion, chopped fine
½ cup finely chopped celery
2 tablespoons minced parsley
1 teaspoon marjoram
1 teaspoon thyme
1 teaspoon salt
¾ cup chopped walnuts
6 cups soft bread crumbs

Melt butter or other fat in large saucepan. Add onion, celery, and seasonings, and cook for 5 minutes. Stir in nut meats and crumbs. Mix well.

224. MEDITERRANEAN BEEF-STUFFED CHICKEN

1-1¼ hours

Medium heat in preheated rotisserie

6 servings

1 whole roasting chicken (4 pounds ready to cook)
Salt
Butter, margarine, or oil

(Serve with cooked wheat, rice, or buckwheat groats)

Wipe bird inside and out, and rub with salt. Stuff. Close
the neck and body openings, and truss. Put chicken on the
spit, and lock with prongs. Brush bird with butter or other
fat, slip the spit into the rotisserie, and roast until crisp.
The chicken is done when drumstick, tested between
thumb and forefinger (hold with paper towel) moves
easily and feels tender. Remove poultry pins or thread,
and carve bird on the spit; start with the drumstick and
continue as usual. Poultry shears are a great convenience.

BEEF STUFFING

1/4 cup butter, margarine, or oil
1 small onion, minced
1/2 pound ground beef
1/2 cup uncooked rice
1/4 cup seedless raisins
3 tablespoons sliced, cooked, peeled chestnuts (optional)
Salt
Pepper
Dash of cinnamon

Heat butter or other fat in large saucepan, add onion, and cook until transparent. Add beef, rice, raisins, chestnuts, salt, pepper, and cinnamon. Let cook for 15 minutes, then stuff as directed above.

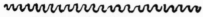

roast
fish
and
shellfish

So many fish and shellfish will take to roasting! Try any firm-fleshed variety: bass, bluefish, cod, haddock, mackerel, pike, for example; and clams, lobsters, large oysters, and shrimp. Use fish with or without head and tail, stuff or not as you wish, but be sure to close any body openings with poultry pins and cord, or sew them up with needle and thread. Tie the fish to the spit with string so it won't break off, and serve on a hot platter with herb, lemon, or anchovy butter, or with wine sauce.

225. HOW TO ROAST FISH

15-25 minutes

Medium heat in preheated rotisserie

Allow ½-¾ pound for each serving

Wash and dry a 3- or 4-pound fish. Leave head and tail on, or remove them. To enhance flavor, sprinkle fish with lemon juice, and refrigerate for an hour or so. Stuff fish if you wish. (See Recipe 140 for Celery Stuffing, or use a recipe of your own.) If you do stuff, close body openings tightly.

Center fish on spit; then tie it with cord so it will not break off. Brush with melted butter, margarine, or other fat, and broil until done. Baste with wine or butter if you wish. Cook until fish is *just* fork-tender—it will fall apart if overdone. Remove string, season with salt and pepper, and serve immediately with pan drippings and additional melted butter.

PASTE MANUFACTURER'S DIRECTIONS
HERE

PASTE MANUFACTURER'S DIRECTIONS HERE

index

A

Almonds, salted, 26
American cheese bites, 19
    pizza, 46
Anchovy fingers, 19
Anything-and-cheese sandwich, 33
Appetizers, *see* Canapés, Hors
        d'oeuvre
Apple
    broil, orange-flavored, 161
    fritters, 159
    macaroon rings, 160
    sandwich, 158
    slices, curried, 158
Apricot sandwich treat, 30
Apricots, 162

B

Bacon, 80
    Canadian-style, 81
    crisps, 23
    pigs-on-a-skewer, 24
    slices, 82
    spit-roast, 191
Bake, lazy-day, 43
Baked Idaho broil, 151
Banana "cake", 43
Bananas, fluted, 162
Barbecued
    beefsteak, 55

broiler, 112
burger in bun, 73
chicken, 192
duck, 192
frankfurters, 91
goose, 192
turkey, 192
spareribs, 190
Beef, *see also* Hamburgers
    best cuts for broiling, 53
    points to remember, 53
    time table, 54
    barbecued, 55
    en brochette, 62
    corned beef hash, 60
    kebabs, 78
    London broil with onion
        sauce, 58
    onion-smothered sirloin, 55
    planked steak for two, 57
    and potatoes Biarritz, 61
    rolled rib roast, 179
    rolled sirloin, 180
    salt-grilled steak, 56
    sizzling broiled steak, 54
Bean and cheese sandwich,
        tangy, 35
Blinis, frozen, 45
    quick homemade, cheese, 45
Bluefish, celery-stuffed, 125
Bologna puff, hearty, 40
Broiler care, 13
Boiled lobster broil, 137
Bread, *see also* Croutons, Toasts
    hot seasoned, 27
    how to reheat, 26

C

D

213

Duck
how to select for roasting, 193
points to remember, 108
Duckling, 119
roast, with orange stuffing, 200

E

Egg, anchovy and mushroom
sandwich, 31
Eggs
grilled, 47
Mornay, 47
in a nest, 31
Eggplant
with anchovies, 146
patties, 145
slices, breaded, 145

F

Figs, Kadota, 164
rice-stuffed, 164
Fish
best kinds for broiling, 122
how to brown, 124
points to remember, 122
celery-stuffed, 125
fillets, 124
flounder fillets in wine sauce, 126
rolled and stuffed, 127
gourmet halibut grill, 129
haddock fillets in herb
butter, 128
lemon-broiled mackerel, 130
planked, 124
roast, 205
salmon steak with broccoli, 131
scrod or pompano amandine, 132
shad roe, 133

steaks, how to broil, 123
trout or smelts meunière, 134
whole or split, 123
Flounder fillets, rolled and
stuffed, 127
in wine sauce, 126
Franks, see Frankfurters
Frankfurters, 89-97
barbecued, 91
broiled, 90
cheese-stuffed, 96
corn-stuffed, 92
and potato Roquefort salad, 93
and tomatoes in open rolls, 94
tropical, on skewers, 95
wiener binge for teen-agers, 97
zesty frank birds, 90
Franks on a pick, 25
French toast, 29
Fritters, apple, 159
pineapple, 169
Frosting, coconut pecan, 163
Fruit ambrosia, 163
Fruits, 157-170
apple broil, orange-flavored, 161
fritters, 159
macaroon rings, 160
sandwich, 158
slices, curried, 158
bananas, fluted, 162
fruit ambrosia, 163
coconut pecan frosting, 163
figs, kadota, 164
rice-stuffed, 164
grapefruit, 4 ways, 165
orange cups, 166
peaches, 4 ways, 167
pears, 4 ways, 168
pineapple, 4 ways, 169
fritters, 169
skewered fruit medley, 170
Fluted broiled bananas, 162
Frozen
blinis, 45
fish, ready to heat, 135
French fried potatoes, 150